Trademark Acknowledgments

All terms mentioned in this book that are known to be trademarks or service marks have been appropriately capitalized. Cisco Press or Cisco Systems, Inc., cannot attest to the accuracy of this information. Use of a term in this book should not be regarded as affecting the validity of any trademark or service mark.

Corporate and Government Sales

The publisher offers excellent discounts on this book when ordered in quantity for bulk purchases or special sales, which may include electronic versions and/or custom covers and content particular to your business, training goals, marketing focus, and branding interests. For more information, please contact:

U.S. Corporate and Government Sales
1-800-382-3419
corpsales@pearsontechgroup.com

For sales outside the United States, please contact:
International Sales
international@pearsoned.com

Feedback Information

At Cisco Press, our goal is to create in-depth technical books of the highest quality and value. Each book is crafted with care and precision, undergoing rigorous development that involves the unique expertise of members from the professional technical community.

Readers' feedback is a natural continuation of this process. If you have any comments regarding how we could improve the quality of this book, or otherwise alter it to better suit your needs, you can contact us through email at feedback@ciscopress.com. Please make sure to include the book title and ISBN in your message.

We greatly appreciate your assistance.

CISCO.

Americas Headquarters
Cisco Systems, Inc.
San Jose, CA

Asia Pacific Headquarters
Cisco Systems (USA) Pte. Ltd.
Singapore

Europe Headquarters
Cisco Systems International BV
Amsterdam, The Netherlands

Cisco has more than 200 offices worldwide. Addresses, phone numbers, and fax numbers are listed on the Cisco Website at www.cisco.com/go/offices.

CCDE, CCENT, Cisco Eos, Cisco HealthPresence, the Cisco logo, Cisco Lumin, Cisco Nexus, Cisco StadiumVision, Cisco TelePresence, Cisco WebEx, DCE, and Welcome to the Human Network are trademarks; Changing the Way We Work, Live, Play, and Learn and Cisco Store are service marks; and Access Registrar, Aironet, AsyncOS, Bringing the Meeting To You, Catalyst, CCDA, CCDP, CCIE, CCIP, CCNA, CCNP, CCSP, CCVP, Cisco, the Cisco Certified Internetwork Expert logo, Cisco IOS, Cisco Press, Cisco Systems, Cisco Systems Capital, the Cisco Systems logo, Cisco Unity, Collaboration Without Limitation, EtherFast, EtherSwitch, Event Center, Fast Step, Follow Me Browsing, FormShare, GigaDrive, HomeLink, Internet Quotient, IOS, iPhone, iQuick Study, IronPort, the IronPort logo, LightStream, Linksys, MediaTone, MeetingPlace, MeetingPlace Chime Sound, MGX, Networkers, Networking Academy, Network Registrar, PCNow, PIX, PowerPanels, ProConnect, ScriptShare, SenderBase, SMARTnet, Spectrum Expert, StackWise, The Fastest Way to Increase Your Internet Quotient, TransPath, WebEx, and the WebEx logo are registered trademarks of Cisco Systems, Inc. and/or its affiliates in the United States and certain other countries.

All other trademarks mentioned in this document or website are the property of their respective owners. The use of the word partner does not imply a partnership relationship between Cisco and any other company. (0812R)

About the Author

Bill Williams is a 16-year information technology veteran. Fourteen of those years have been with Cisco Systems, where he has held several leadership positions. Currently, Bill is a regional manager for data center and virtualization technologies, covering the service provider market segment. In 2008, 2010, and 2011, Bill lead the top-producing service provider regions in the United States and Canada. In 2010, Bill won the Manager Excellence award.

Bill attended the University of North Carolina at Chapel Hill and holds master's degrees from Harvard Divinity School and the UNC Kenan-Flagler Business School. Bill also holds U.S. Patent 7260590 for a content delivery application.

The Economics of Cloud Computing is Bill's second book for Cisco Press. *The Business Case for Storage Networks* was published in 2004.

Bill lives with his wife and children in Chapel Hill, North Carolina.

Dedication

This book is dedicated to Lia, Isabel, Lee, and Catherine. To the Dream Team: Thank you for making it all worthwhile.

Acknowledgments

First and foremost, I'd like to thank my manager and friend, Curt Reid, for his support and guidance throughout this process. Curt, your continued leadership and thoughtful insights will always remain priceless in my book.

To my team, the hardest-working people in show business, thank you for your tireless dedication to the task at hand.

A special thank-you goes to Toby Ford for his commentary and guidance in thinking through the longer-term impact of cloud computing. The world is waiting for your book, Toby.

A huge thank-you goes out to George Reese and Stuart Neumann. George's book, *Cloud Application Architectures: Building Applications and Infrastructure in the Cloud*, and Stuart's research at Verdantix on carbon emissions and cloud computing were both instrumental in the thought process behind the book you now hold in your hand. Gentlemen, I cannot thank you enough for your help.

Finally, I must also thank my closest peers and advisors in the industry: Jon Beck, James Christopher, Dominick Delfino, Insa Elliot, Melissa Hinde, Jason Hoffman, Jonathan King, Paul Werner, Ted Stein, Phil Lowden, Dante Malagrino, Frank Palumbo, and Rafi Yahalom. You are all guiding lights in a field filled with stars.

The Economics of Cloud Computing

Bill Williams

Cisco Press

800 East 96th Street
Indianapolis, Indiana 46240 USA

The Economics of Cloud Computing

Bill Williams

Copyright© 2012 Cisco Systems, Inc.

Published by:
Cisco Press
800 East 96th Street
Indianapolis, IN 46240 USA

Printed in the United States of America

First Printing June 2012

Library of Congress Cataloging-in-Publication Data:

Williams, Bill, 1970-
   The economics of cloud computing / Bill Williams.
      p. cm.
   Includes bibliographical references and index.
   ISBN 978-1-58714-306-9 (pbk. : alk. paper) — ISBN 1-58714-306-2 (pbk. : alk. paper)
   1. Cloud computing. 2. Information technology—Economic aspects. I. Title.

   QA76.585.W55 2012
   004.6782—dc23

ISBN-13: 978-1-58714-306-9

ISBN-10: 1-58714-306-2

Warning and Disclaimer

This book is designed to provide information about the economic impact of cloud computing adoption. Every effort has been made to make this book as complete and as accurate as possible, but no warranty or fitness is implied.

The information is provided on an "as is" basis. The author, Cisco Press, and Cisco Systems, Inc. shall have neither liability nor responsibility to any person or entity with respect to any loss or damages arising from the information contained in this book or from the use of the discs or programs that may accompany it.

The opinions expressed in this book belong to the author and are not necessarily those of Cisco Systems, Inc.

Publisher
Paul Boger

Associate Publisher
Dave Dusthimer

Business Operation Manager, Cisco Press
Anand Sundaram

Manager Global Certification
Erik Ullanderson

Executive Editor
Mary Beth Ray

Managing Editor
Sandra Schroeder

Senior Project Editor
Tonya Simpson

Copy Editor
John Edwards

Editorial Assistant
Vanessa Evans

Cover Designer
Sandra Schroeder

Composition
Mark Shirar

Indexer
Cheryl Lenser

Proofreader
Sheri Cain

CONTENTS AT A GLANCE

CONTENTS

Foreword

Depending on whom you talk to, cloud computing is either very old or very new. Many cloud computing technologies date back to the 1960s. In fact, it's very hard to point to any single technology and say, "That new thing there is cloud computing." However, cloud adoption—public, private, or otherwise—is a new phenomenon, and the roots of that adoption lie in the economics of cloud computing.

Companies have historically consumed technology as capital expenditure "bursts" combined with fixed operational costs. When you needed a new system, you would finance it separately from your operational budget. The 2000s brought us a one/two punch that challenged that traditional consumption model.

First, the recession in 2001/2002 resulted in a huge downsizing of corporate IT. By the middle of the decade, corporate IT had evolved into a tremendously efficient component of the business. These efficiency gains, however, came at the cost of IT's ability to support strategic business endeavors.

The second punch came in the form of the financial system collapse of 2008. As a result of this economic shock, even the largest companies found it difficult to gain access to affordable capital for new IT projects—or any other capital expenditure, for that matter. Not only did IT now lack the bandwidth to support strategic endeavors, but it also lacked any source of funding to support them.

In 2008 and 2009, the economics of cloud computing were a black-and-white world supporting the simplistic statements, "OPEX good, CAPEX bad" and "public cloud cheap, traditional IT expensive." Q4 2008 and Q1 2009 were parts of an extreme economic situation in which these rules of thumb were more true than not. In fact, I got into cloud computing specifically because capital was so hard to find.

I had a marketing company called Valtira that was working on a new on-demand product offering. The capital expense for this project was insane, and it wasn't clear that the product offering would succeed. We moved into the Amazon cloud in early 2008 (before the crisis hit, but with capital scarce for small companies) to develop this product offering and test it. The advantage of the cloud to us was simple: Without any up-front investment, we could test out a new product offering. If it succeeded, we'd be thrilled to continue spending the money to support its ongoing operations. If it failed, we'd kill it and only be out a few thousand dollars.

In other words, the economics of cloud computing enabled us to take on a strategic project in a weakening economic climate that would never have seen the light of day in a traditional IT setting. That's the true economics of cloud computing.

While it might seem silly from today's economic perspective, the "OPEX good, CAPEX bad" mantra combined with IT's diminished capacity to be a strategic partner in business drove marketers, engineers, salespeople, and HR away from IT into the arms of cloud computing vendors. After these business units tasted the freedom of cloud computing, they have almost always resisted a return to a world in which IT is the gatekeeper to all technology.

Another simplistic idea from the "early days" of cloud computing is that the cloud is cheaper than traditional computing. In many cases, a cloud solution will be cheaper in isolation than a comparable traditional solution. The complex reality is that the agility of cloud computing will result in greater consumption of technology than would occur in a traditional IT infrastructure. The overall costs of the cloud are thus almost always higher—but that can be a good thing!

These simplistic memes about cloud computing economics survive today in spite of the much more complex reality. A strategy based on them is certain to result in unachievable expectations and failed attempts at cloud adoption. Although the comparison of capital expenses versus operational expenses plays a role in this calculus, so many other factors are more important these days. Understanding the true economics of cloud computing is absolutely critical to a mature cloud computing strategy and overall success in the cloud.

— George Reese

Introduction

In my conversations with customers, partners, and peers, one topic seems to bubble to the surface more than any other: How do I financially justify the move to the cloud?

Initially, the notion of a business case for cloud computing seemed almost redundant. It seemed to me that the cost savings associated with cloud computing were self-evident and therefore no further explanation was needed. Based on my conversations with people in the industry—consumers, providers, and manufacturers of IT goods and services—cloud adoption appeared to be a foregone conclusion. Based on the data, cloud implementation was either already well under way or was on the near-term priority list of most IT leaders worldwide.

Yet the reality is otherwise. For many people, the actual journey to the cloud is still fraught with uncertainty and confusion. Spending money on IT services provided *externally*—especially when companies invest millions of dollars a year to implement and operate hardware and software *internally* as part of a long-standing, integrated IT supply chain—crosses a major psychological boundary.

This psychological hurdle, coupled with all the various political implications of "build versus buy" decisions, makes the financial justification of cloud adoption all the more imperative.

Goals and Methods

The most important goal of this book is to help you understand—from an economic standpoint—both the short-term and long-term impacts of cloud computing.

We are in the middle of a major technological and sociological revolution, one that will take years to fully unfold. Evidence of this revolution is everywhere and nowhere all at once. For example, we can now access millions of titles of streamed content from multiple devices in our homes, including tablet computers and smartphones. At the same time, however, the servers that process and distribute this data are quickly becoming invisible. Server virtualization, the primary technical driver for cloud computing, has essentially dissolved the concept of a physical server. In the last 40 years, servers have very literally morphed from massive "big iron" mainframes to nothing more than central processing units (CPU) and memory driven by the network.

Economics—"the dismal science"—is a broad topic touching nearly every aspect of human society. It would be supremely arrogant (if not impossible) to do a thorough economic analysis of how cloud computing will change the world as we know it in an executive-level overview designed for the mainstream reader.

There are a number of pure scientists—professional economists, researchers, and educators (like Federico Etro)—who are far more qualified and proficient at this type of analysis and explication. Etro's work (alongside several others listed in Appendix A) is recommended for readers interested in going two or three (or even *N*) layers beneath the surface.

If you know nothing about cloud computing or finance and you walk away at the end of this book with a fundamental understanding of cloud service and deployment models, of basic financial metrics, and how to apply these concepts together in a business case methodology, I will consider my primary objectives met.

If, on the other hand, you have more than a cursory understanding of cloud computing and the impact the cloud has on IT budgeting and finance, and if you are steeped in both ITIL and capital-budgeting methodologies, feel free to fast-forward. Feel free to fast-forward and imagine how we, as a networked, interconnected global society, can best leverage the extreme economies of scale associated with cloud computing. Imagine how—as the adoption of cloud computing accelerates over the coming years—we can best utilize the power of ubiquitous (and nearly free) computing. If you participate in this thought experiment and share in the ongoing dialogue concerning "the cloud economy," I will consider this effort a success overall.

Who Should Read This Book

This book is meant to serve as a primer on the financial and economic impacts of cloud computing. As such, anyone responsible for making decisions regarding IT solutions and platforms can find value here.

Individuals who work in IT procurement, legal, and finance—persons whose roles are already being impacted by the shift to cloud computing—might be interested in understanding more clearly how the technological revolution that is cloud computing fits in a broader social and historical context.

Finally, people who consider themselves well-versed in the nomenclature and business of cloud computing—people who live, eat, sleep, and breathe the cloud—can be challenged to think more deeply about the potential social and global benefits of cheap and ubiquitous computing.

While my primary concern is to enable good decision-making with respect to adopting cloud platforms, it is my hope that the economic surplus that stems from cloud computing can and will be put to extraordinary use.

How This Book Is Organized

This book is designed to be read straight through, ideally in one sitting. Accordingly, it is concise—only four chapters—and organized in such a manner as to enable you to put the information straight to work.

The core of the book (Chapters 1 through 4) covers the following material:

- **Chapter 1, "What Is Cloud Computing?—The Journey to Cloud":** This chapter defines cloud computing service and deployment models and outlines many common characteristics of clouds. Additionally, this chapter introduces two concepts—the *IT supply chain* and the *value chain*—that can be used to baseline IT costs and justify the investment in cloud computing technologies.

- **Chapter 2, "Metrics That Matter—What You Need to Know":** This chapter introduces concepts essential to the financial analysis and justification of IT solutions. Critical business value measurements are broken into two categories: *indirect metrics* and *direct metrics*. Total cost of ownership (TCO), time to market, opportunity costs, churn rate, productivity, and others are introduced as *indirect metrics*. Payback method, net present value (NPV), return on investment (ROI), return on equity (ROE), and economic value added (EVA) are covered as *direct metrics*.

- **Chapter 3, "Sample Case Studies—Applied Metrics":** This chapter applies the *indirect* and *direct metrics* from Chapter 2 to the implementation of cloud computing solutions and platforms at a fictional startup in the pharmaceutical industry. Software as a Service (SaaS), Infrastructure as a Service (IaaS), and Platform as a Service (PaaS) examples are discussed.

- **Chapter 4, "The Cloud Economy—The Human-Economic Impact of Cloud Computing":** This chapter covers technological revolutions and paradigm changes as related to human development. Analysis in this chapter pertains to cloud computing as both an economic enabler (for established and emerging economies alike) and as a driver for global sustainability.

The supplemental materials include

- **Appendix A, "References":** Included here are books, articles, and papers that are either cited in this manuscript or were consulted during my research.

- **Appendix B, "Decision Maker's Checklist":** Included here are items to consider when choosing to purchase and implement cloud solutions.

- **Glossary:** Commonly used terms and phrases related to cloud computing are defined herein.

1

What Is Cloud Computing?—The Journey to Cloud

This chapter begins with a definition of cloud computing before providing an in-depth look at the following topics:

- *Cloud Service Models*
- *Cloud Deployment Models*

In this chapter, we also compare IT and application delivery processes to manufacturing supply chains. The introduction of Michael Porter's concept of the value chain will be helpful in understanding the IT cost center. Both the supply chain analogy and the value chain concept are used in future chapters to establish a baseline for cost analysis for IT deliverables. Understanding the IT supply chain will in turn simplify the process of cost justification for cloud-computing adoption.

It is often joked that if you ask five people to define cloud computing, you will get ten different definitions. Generally speaking, we seem to want to overcomplicate cloud computing and what the cloud means in real life. While in some cases, there can be complex technologies involved behind the scenes, there is nothing inherently complex about cloud computing.

In fact, the technology behind cloud computing is by and large the easy part. Frankly, the hardest part of cloud computing is the people. The politics of migrating from legacy platforms to the cloud is inherently complicated because the adoption of cloud computing affects the way many people—not just IT professionals—do their jobs. Over time, cloud computing might drastically change some roles so that they are no longer recognizable from their current form, or even potentially eliminate some jobs entirely. Thus, the human-economic implications of adopting and migrating to cloud computing platforms and processes should not be taken lightly.

There are also, of course, countless benefits stemming from the adoption of cloud computing, both in the short term and the longer term. Many benefits of cloud computing in the corporate arena are purely financial, while other network externalities relating to cloud computing will have much broader positive effects. The ubiquity of free or inexpensive computing accessed through the cloud is already impacting both communications in First World and established economies, and research and development, agriculture, and banking in Third World and emerging economies.

Therefore, it is important for decision makers to understand the impact of cloud computing both from a financial and from a sociological standpoint. This understanding begins with a clear definition of cloud computing.

Cloud Computing Defined

Cloud computing is not one single technology, nor is it one single architecture. Cloud computing is essentially the next phase of innovation and adoption of a platform for computing, networking, and storage technologies designed to provide rapid time to market and drastic cost reductions. (We talk more about adoption and innovation cycles in the scope of economic development in Chapter 4, "The Cloud Economy—The Human-Economic Impact of Cloud Computing.")

There have been both incremental and exponential advances made in computing, networking, and storage over the last several years, but only recently have these advancements—coupled with the financial drivers related to economic retraction and recession—reached a tipping point, creating a major market shift toward cloud adoption.

The business workflows (the rules and processes behind business functions like accounts payable and accounts receivable) in use in corporations today are fairly commonplace. With the exception of relatively recent changes required to support regulatory compliance—Sarbanes-Oxley (SOX), Payment Card Industry Data Security Standard (PCI DSS), or the Health Insurance Portability and Accountability Act (HIPAA), for example—most software functions required to pay bills, make payroll, process purchase orders, and so on have remained largely unchanged for many years.

Similarly, the underlying technologies of cloud computing have been in use in some form or another for decades. Virtualization, for example—arguably the biggest technology driver behind cloud computing—is almost 40 years old. Virtualization—the logical abstraction of hardware through a layer of software—has been in use since the mainframe era.[1] Just as server and storage vendors have been using different types of virtualization for nearly four decades, virtualization has become equally commonplace in the corporate network: It would be almost impossible to find a LAN today that does not use VLAN functionality.

In the same way that memory and network virtualization have standardized over time, server virtualization solutions—such as those offered by Microsoft, VMware, Parallels, and Xen—and the virtual machine, or VM, have become the fundamental building blocks of the cloud.

Over the last few decades, the concept of a computer and its role in corporate and academic environments have changed very little, while the physical, tangible reality of the computer has changed greatly: Processing power has more than doubled every two years while the physical footprint of a computer has dramatically decreased (think mainframe versus handheld).[2]

Moore's Law aside, at its most basic level, the CPU takes I/O and writes it to RAM and/or to a hard drive. This simple function allows applications to create, process, and save mission-critical data. Radically increased speed and performance, however, means that this function can be performed faster than ever before and at massive scale. Additionally, new innovations and enhancements to these existing technology paradigms (hypervisor-bypass and Cisco Extended Memory Technology, for example) are changing our concepts of what a computer is and does. (Where should massive amounts of data reside during processing? What functions should the network interface card perform?) This material and functional evolution, coupled with economic and business drivers, are spurring a dramatic market shift toward the cloud and the anticipated creation and growth of many new markets.

---

1. "The Virtualization Reality: Are hypervisors the new foundation for system software?" Simon Crosby, Xensource and David Brown, Sun Microsystems. Accessed January 2012, http://queue.acm.org/detail.cfm?id=1189289.

2. "Variations of Moore's Law have been applied to improvement over time in disk drive capacity, display resolution, and network bandwidth. In these and many other cases of digital improvement, doubling happens both quickly and reliably." Brynjolfsson, Erik; McAfee, Andrew (2011-10-17). *Race Against The Machine: How the Digital Revolution is Accelerating Innovation, Driving Productivity, and Irreversibly Transforming Employment and the Economy (Kindle Locations 286-289)*. Digital Frontier Press. Kindle Edition.

While it is fair to say that what is truly new about the cloud is the use of innovative and interrelated technologies to solve complex business problems in novel ways, that is not the whole story. Perhaps what is most promising about cloud computing, aside from the breadth of solutions currently available and the functionality and scalability of new and emerging platforms, is the massive potential for future products and solutions developed in and for the cloud. The untapped potential of the cloud and the externalities stemming from consumer and corporate adoption of cloud computing can create significant benefits for both developed and underdeveloped economies.

With a basic understanding of the technology and market drivers behind cloud computing, it is appropriate to move forward with a deeper discussion of what cloud computing means in real life. To do this, we turn to the National Institute of Standards and Technology (NIST).

NIST Definition of Cloud Computing

For the record, here is the definition of cloud computing offered by the National Institute of Standards and Technology (NIST):

> Cloud computing is a model for enabling convenient, on-demand network access to a shared pool of configurable computing resources (e.g., networks, servers, storage, applications, and services) that can be rapidly provisioned and released with minimal management effort or service provider interaction.[3]

This definition is considered the gold standard of definitions for cloud computing, and if we unpack it, we can see why. First, note that cloud computing is a usage model and not a technology. There are multiple different flavors of cloud computing, each with its own distinctive traits and advantages. Using this definition, *cloud computing* is an umbrella term highlighting the similarities and differences in each deployment model while avoiding being prescriptive about the particular technologies required to implement or support a certain platform.

Second, we can see that cloud computing is based on a pool of network, compute, storage, and application resources. Here, we have the first premise for the business value analysis and metrics we use in later chapters. Typically speaking, a total cost of ownership (TCO) analysis starts with tallying the costs of each of the combined elements necessary in a solution. Just like the TCO of automobile ownership includes the cost of gas and maintenance, the TCO of a computing solution includes the cost of software licenses, upgrades, and expansions, as well as power consumption. Just as we will analyze the TCO of the computing status quo (that is, the legacy or noncloud model), treating all the resources in the data center as a pool will enable us to more

---

3. National Institute of Standards and Technology, "NIST Definition of Cloud Computing," www.nist.gov/itl/cloud/upload/cloud-def-v15.pdf, accessed December 2011.

accurately quantify the business value of cloud computing as a solution at each stage of implementation.

Finally, we see that the fundamental benefits of cloud computing are provisioning speed and ease of use. Here is the next premise on which we will base the business value analysis for choosing cloud computing platforms: time to market (TTM) and reduction of operational expenditures (OPEX).

OPEX reductions related to provisioning costs—the costs associated with moves, adds, changes (MAC) necessary to provide and support a computing solution—coupled with reducing the time to implement (TTI) a platform are the principal cost benefits of cloud computing. The former is a measure of reducing ongoing expenses, while the latter is a measure of how quickly we can generate the benefits related to implementing a solution.

Whether it is a revenue-generating application, as in the case of a service provider monitoring network performance, or whether it is a business-critical platform supporting, say, accounts receivable, the measurements used to quantify the associated benefits are essentially the same.

Characteristics of Clouds

The NIST definition also highlights five essential characteristics of cloud computing:

- Broad network access
- On-demand self-service
- Resource pooling
- Measured service
- Rapid elasticity[4]

Let's step through these concepts individually.

First, we cover *broad network access*. Access to resources in the cloud is available over multiple device types. This not only includes the most common devices (laptops, workstations, and so on) but also mobile phones, thin clients, and the like. Contrast broad network access with access to compute and network resources during the mainframe era. Compute resources 40 years ago were scarce and costly. To conserve those resources, usage was limited based on priority and criticality of workloads. Similarly, network resources were also scarce. IP-based networks were not in prevalent usage four decades ago; consequently, access to ubiquitous high-bandwidth, low-latency networks did not exist. Over time, costs associated with the

---

4. National Institute of Standards and Technology, "NIST Definition of Cloud Computing," www.nist.gov/itl/cloud/upload/cloud-def-v15.pdf, accessed December 2011.

network (like costs associated with computing and storage) have decreased because of manufacturing scalability, commoditization of associated technologies, and competition in the marketplace. As network bandwidth has increased, network access and scalability have also increased accordingly. Broad network access can and should be seen both as a trait of cloud computing and as an enabler.

On-demand self-service is a key—some say the primary—characteristic of the cloud. Think of IT as a complex supply chain with the application and the end user at the tail end of the chain. In noncloud environments, the ability to self-provision resources fundamentally disrupts most (if not all) of the legacy processes of corporate IT. This includes workflow related to procurement and provisioning of storage, servers, network nodes, software licenses, and so on.

Historically, capacity planning has been performed in "silos" or in isolated organizational structures with little or no communication between decision makers and stakeholders. In noncloud or legacy environments, when the end user can self-provision without interacting with the provider, the downstream result is usually extreme inefficiency and waste.

 Note

In his classic *Competitive Advantage: Creating and Sustaining Superior Performance*, Michael Porter outlined the concept of the *value chain*. Porter's work highlights how firms can increase their competitive advantage by understanding and optimizing the support and operational functions related to bringing products to market.

In short, Porter breaks down the functional components of the firm into fundamental building blocks: *primary* and *support activities*. Primary activities include inbound and outbound logistics, operations, service, and sales and marketing. Support activities include processes like procurement and human resources. Within primary and support activities, there are *direct, indirect*, and *quality assurance* activities that directly create value, indirectly contribute to value creation, or ensure the quality of other processes.[5] Each of these are areas that are touched or will be touched by the adoption of cloud computing.

Porter analyzes economies and diseconomies of scale related to value chain activities, indicating that economies of scale increase with both operating efficiencies and capacity utilization.[6] Analysis of the IT supply chain and the use of simple cost-accounting methodologies will show that adoption of cloud computing can positively influence operational efficiency and capacity utilization, and thereby increase economies of scale.

---

5. Michael E. Porter, *Competitive Advantage: Creating and Sustaining Superior Performance*, The Free Press, New York, 1985, pp. 41–44.

6. Ibid, p. 70.

Self-provisioning in noncloud environments causes legacy processes and functions—such as capacity planning, network management (providing quality of service [QoS]), and security (management of firewalls and access control lists [ACL])—to grind to a halt or even break down completely. The well-documented "bullwhip effect" in supply chain management—when incomplete or inaccurate information results in high variability in production costs—applies not only to manufacturing environments but also to the provisioning of IT resources in noncloud environments.[7]

Cloud-based architectures, however, are designed and built with self-provisioning in mind. This premise implies the use of fairly sophisticated software frameworks and portals to manage provisioning and back-office functions. Historically, the lack of commercial off-the-shelf (COTS) software purpose-built for cloud automation led many companies to build their own frameworks to support these processes. While many companies do still use homegrown portals, adoption of COTS software packages designed to manage and automate enterprise workloads has increased as major ISVs and startups alike find ways to differentiate their solutions.

Resource pooling is a fundamental premise of scalability in the cloud. Without pooled computing, networks, and storage, a service provider must provision across multiple silos (discrete, independent resources with few or no interconnections.) Multitenant environments, where multiple customers share adjacent resources in the cloud with their peers, are the basis of public cloud infrastructures. With multitenancy, there is an inherent increase in operational expenditures, which can be mitigated by certain hardware configurations and software solutions, such as application and server profiles.

Imagine a telephone network that is not multitenant. This is extremely difficult to do: It would imply dedicated circuits from end to end, all the way from the provider to each and every consumer. Now imagine the expense: not only the exorbitant capital costs of the dedicated hardware but also the operating expenses associated with maintenance. Simple troubleshooting processes would require an operator to authenticate into multiple thousands of systems just to verify access. If a broader system issue affected more than one network, the mean time to recovery (MTTR) would be significant. Without resource pooling and multitenancy, the economics of cloud computing do not make financial sense.

Measured service implies that usage of these pooled resources is monitored and reported to the consumer, providing visibility into rates of consumption and associated costs. Accurate measurement of resource consumption, for the purposes of

---

7. The bullwhip effect and supply chain management have been widely studied and documented. "The Bullwhip Effect in Supply Chains," by Hau L. Lee, V. Padmanabhan, and Seungjin Whang, is a classic in this field. MIT Sloan Management Review, http://sloanreview.mit.edu/the-magazine/1997-spring/3837/the-bullwhip-effect-in-supply-chains/, accessed December 2011.

chargeback (or merely for cross-departmental reporting and planning), has long been a wish-list item for IT stakeholders. Building and supporting a system capable of such granular reporting, however, has always been a tall order.

As computing resources moved from the command-and-control world of the main-frame (where measurement and reporting software was built in to the system) to the controlled chaos of open systems and client-server platforms (where measurement and reporting were bolted on as an afterthought, if at all), visibility into costs and consumption has become increasingly limited. Frequently enough, IT teams have built systems to monitor the usage of one element (the CPU, for example) while using COTS software for another element (perhaps storage).

Tying the two systems together, however, across a large enterprise often becomes a full-time effort. If chargeback is actually implemented, it becomes imperative to drop everything else when the COTS vendor releases a patch or an upgrade; other-wise, access to reporting data is lost. Assuming that usage accounting and report-ing are handled accordingly, billing then becomes yet another internal IT function requiring management and full-time equivalent (FTE) resources. Measured service, in terms of the cloud, takes the majority of the above effort out of the equation, thereby dramatically reducing the associated operational expense.

The final trait highlighted in the NIST definition of cloud computing is *rapid elas-ticity*. Elastic resources are critical to reducing costs and decreasing time to market (TTM). Indeed, the notion of elastic computing in the IT supply chain is so desir-able that Amazon even named its cloud platform Elastic Compute Cloud (EC2). As I demonstrate in later chapters, the majority of the costs associated with deploying applications stems from provisioning (moves, adds, and changes, or MAC) in the IT supply chain. Therefore, simplifying the provisioning process can generate significant cost reductions and enable faster revenue generation.

Think of the workflow and business processes related to the provisioning of a simple application. Whether the application is for external customers or for internal employees, the provisioning processes are often similar (if not identical.) The costs associated with a delayed customer release, however, can be significantly higher. The opportunity costs of a delayed customer-facing application in a highly competitive market can be exorbitant, particularly in terms of customer acquisition and reten-tion. In short, the stakes are much higher with respect to bringing revenue-generating applications to market. We look at different methods of measuring the impact of time-to-market in Chapter2, "Metrics That Matter—What You Need to Know."

For a simple application (either internal or external) the typical workflow will look something like the following. Disk storage requirements are gathered prompting the storage workflow—logical unit number (LUN) provisioning and masking, file system creation, and so on. A database is created and disks are allocated. Users are created on the server and the associated database, and privileges are assigned based on roles and responsibilities. Server and application access is granted on the network based on ACLs and IP address assignments.

At each step of this process functional owners (network, storage, and server administrators) have the opportunity to preprovision resources in advance of upcoming requests. Unfortunately, there is also the opportunity for functional owners to overprovision to limit the frequency of requests and to mitigate delays in the supply chain.

Overprovisioning in any one function, however, can also lead to deprivation and delays in the next function, thereby igniting the aforementioned bullwhip effect.[8] The costs associated with the bullwhip effect in a typical IT supply chain can be significant. Waste associated with poor resource utilization can easily cost multiple millions of dollars a year in a medium to large enterprise. Delays in deprovisioning unused or unneeded resources also add to this waste factor, increasing poor utilization rates. Imagine the expense of a hotel with no capability to book rooms. That unlikely scenario occurs frequently in IT when projects are cancelled or discontinued. Legacy funding models assume allocated capital expenditures (CAPEX) are constantly in use, always generating a return. The reality is otherwise: The capability to quickly decommission and reassign hardware outside the cloud does not exist, so costly resources can remain idle much of their useful lives.

In a cloud-based architecture, resources can be provisioned so quickly as to appear unlimited to the consumer. If there is one single hallmark trait of the cloud, it is likely this one: the ability to flatten the IT supply chain to provision applications in a matter of minutes instead of days or weeks.

Of these essential characteristics, the fifth—rapid elasticity, or the ability to quickly provision and deprovision—is perhaps the most critical in terms of cost savings relative to legacy architectures.

The NIST definition also includes the notion of *service* and *deployment* models. For a more complete picture of what is meant by the term *cloud computing*, it is necessary to spend a few minutes with these concepts.

Cloud Service Models

- Software as a Service (SaaS)
- Platform as a Service (PaaS)
- Infrastructure as a Service (IaaS)

---

8. An in-depth analysis of the bullwhip effect in manufacturing, wholesale, and retail can be found at http://opim.wharton.upenn.edu/~cachon/pdf/bwv2.pdf.

Cachon, Randall, and Schmidt: "In Search of the Bullwhip Effect," *Manufacturing & Service Operations Management 9(4)*, pp. 457–479. INFORMS, accessed January 2012.

Software as a Service

Software as a Service (SaaS) is the cloud service model with which most individuals are familiar, even if they do not consider themselves cloud-savvy. Google's Gmail, for example, is one of the most widely known and commonly used SaaS platforms existing today.

SaaS, simply put, is the ability to use a software package on someone else's infrastructure. Gmail differs from typical corporate email platforms like Microsoft Exchange in that the hardware and the software supporting the mail service do not live on corporate-owned, IT-managed servers—the infrastructure supporting Gmail belongs to Google. The ability to use email without implementing expensive hardware and complex software on-site offers great flexibility (and cost reductions) to even small- and medium-sized businesses.

Customer relationship management (CRM) SaaS packages such as Salesforce.com also have significant adoption rates in corporate environments for exactly the same reasons. The increased adoption rate of SaaS in corporate IT stems from SaaS platforms' ability to provide all the benefits of a complex software package while mitigating (if not eliminating entirely) the challenges seen with legacy software environments.[9]

We look at a specific example in Chapter 3, "Sample Case Studies—Applied Metrics," but consider the following: SaaS models enable customers to use vendors' software without the CAPEX associated with the hardware required to run the platform, and without the OPEX associated with managing that hardware. Significant OPEX reductions are also related to the elimination of ongoing maintenance and support. For example, using a SaaS model, when a new release of the software is available, it can simply be pushed out "over the wire," removing the need for complex upgrades, which normally would require hours of FTE time to test and implement.

Infrastructure as a Service

Infrastructure as a Service (IaaS) can almost be seen as the inverse of Software as a Service. With an IaaS model, the service provider delivers the necessary hardware resources (network, compute, storage) required to run a customer's applications.

---

9. The costs associated with ERP implementations have been researched and documented heavily. Of particular note are the implications for developing countries. See Huang, Z. and Palvia, P. "ERP Implementation Issues in Advanced and Developing Countries." *Business Process Management Journal.* Vol 7, No 3, 2001, pp. 276–284. See also "Why ERP may not be Suitable for Organisations in Developing Countries in Asia," by Rajapakse, Jayanatha, and Seddon, Peter B.

Service providers who have built their businesses on colocation services are typically inclined to offer IaaS cloud service models. Colocation service providers (such as Terremark's NAP of the Americas, Switch and Data, and Level 3, as well as many others) have significant investments in networking infrastructure designed to provide high-bandwidth connectivity for services such as video, voice, and peering.[10]

IaaS service models allow customers to take advantage of these massively scalable networks and data centers at a fraction of the cost associated with building and managing their own infrastructures.

Platform as a Service

Finally, Platform as a Service (PaaS) is best described as a development environment hosted on third-party infrastructure to facilitate rapid design, testing, and deployment of new applications. PaaS environments are often used as application "sandboxes," where developers are free to create (and in a sense improvise) in an environment where the cost of consuming resources is greatly reduced.

Google App Engine, VMware's SpringSource, and Amazon's Amazon Web Services (AWS) are common examples of PaaS offerings. PaaS service models offer customers the ability to quickly build, test, and release software products—with often complex requirements for add-on services—using infrastructure that is purpose-built for application development. Adopting PaaS service models thereby eliminates the need for costly infrastructure buildup and teardown typically seen in most corporate development environments.

Given the increased demand for new smartphone applications, it should come as no surprise that of the three cloud computing service models, PaaS currently has the highest growth rate.[11]

Cloud Deployment Models

To close out our discussion of what cloud computing is and is not, we should review one more element highlighted in the NIST definition of cloud computing: deployment models.

---

10. The Colocation Service Provider Directory, www.colocationprovider.org/whatiscolocation.htm, accessed December 2011.

11. 7Economy Global Economy Library, "Cloud Computing: PaaS: Application Development and Deployment Platform in the Cloud," http://7economy.com/archives/6857, accessed December 2011.

Our gold standard of cloud computing definitions calls out the following deployment models:

- Private cloud
- Community cloud
- Public cloud
- Hybrid cloud

Let us briefly walk through each of these models.

Private Cloud

Using the notion of "siloed infrastructures," many corporate IT environments today could be considered private clouds in that they are designed and built by and for a single customer to support specific functions critical for the success of a single line of business.

In today's parlance, however, a private cloud might or might not be hosted on the customer's premises. Correspondingly, a customer implementing his own private cloud on-premise might not achieve the financial benefits of a private cloud offered by a service provider that has built a highly scalable cloud solution. An in-depth analysis of costs associated with legacy platforms should highlight the differences between today's private clouds and yesterday's legacy silos.

It should also go without saying that legacy silos are not true private clouds because they do not embody the five essential characteristics we outlined earlier.

Community Cloud

In a community cloud model, more than one group with common and specific needs shares the cloud infrastructure. This can include environments such as a U.S. federal agency cloud with stringent security requirements, or a health and medical cloud with regulatory and policy requirements for privacy matters. There is no mandate for the infrastructure to be either on-site or off-site to qualify as a community cloud.

Public Cloud

The public cloud deployment model is what is most often thought of as a cloud, in that it is multitenant capable and is shared by a number of customers/consumers who likely have nothing in common. Amazon, Apple, Microsoft, and Google, to name but a few, all offer public cloud services.

Hybrid Cloud

A hybrid cloud deployment is simply a combination of two or more of the previous deployment models with a management framework in place so that the environments appear as a single cloud, typically for the purposes of "cloud peering" or "bursting." Expect demand for hybrid cloud solutions in environments where strong require- ments for security or regulatory compliance exist alongside requirements for price and performance.

Note that major cloud providers typically offer one or more of these types of deployment and service models. For example, Amazon AWS offers both PaaS and public cloud services. Terremark offers private and community clouds with spe- cialized hybrid cloud offerings, colocation and exchange point services, and cost- efficient public cloud services through vCloud Express.[12]

 Note

> To determine the best cloud offering for your business, it is important to understand (or at least have a good idea of) your compute, storage, and net- working requirements. It is helpful to know your budget and your total cost of ownership (TCO) metrics as well. Cloud computing providers will work with you to help you scope your environments for the purposes of sizing and capacity planning. Most providers will even help you determine an estimated return on investment (ROI) for your migration to the cloud.
>
> While it is important for you to understand your infrastructure requirements, it is most critical for you to understand both your business processes and goals, and your underlying application architecture.
>
> A strong knowledge of your critical data—where it lives and how you use it for business-critical decisions and customer success—will enable you to make a well-informed choice about cloud platforms and solutions.

Conclusion

In this chapter, we explored the standard definition of cloud computing to establish a baseline of common terminology. Understanding the essential characteristics of cloud computing platforms, as well as cloud deployment and service models, is criti- cal for making informed decisions and for choosing the appropriate platform for your business needs.

---

12. See Terremark's most recent 10-K filing: www.faqs.org/sec-filings/100614/ TERREMARK-WORLDWIDE-INC_10-K/.

Additionally in this chapter, we introduced Michael Porter's concept of the value chain and drew a comparison among IT infrastructure, application deployments, and manufacturing supply chains. These concepts are key components for understanding the costs (both CAPEX and OPEX) associated with traditional or legacy systems and the offsets potentially achieved by migrating to the cloud.

In the next chapter, we look at the business metrics most often used to measure the impact of technology adoption and implementation.

2

Metrics That Matter— What You Need to Know

This chapter introduces the following topics:

- Business Value Measurements
- Indirect and Direct Metrics
- Total Cost of Ownership

In this chapter, we focus on understanding total cost of ownership (TCO) and other key performance indicators for business and IT. After revisiting the IT supply chain analogy, we establish a framework for measuring the financial value of critical components in an IT system. This baseline will allow us to use capital planning and budgeting tools to estimate the business value of moving IT services to a cloud computing platform.

Business Value Measurements

In this section, we examine the process of measuring the business value of IT. While it is relatively easy to measure overall business performance using the language of profits and losses—and the reporting methodologies dictated by the Financial Accounting Standards Boards (FASB) and Generally Accepted Accounting Principles (GAAP)—it is usually not as simple to measure the performance of any one distinct function inside of a business entity.

Just as there are *direct* and *indirect costs* associated with a project or a product, and—as we saw with Michael Porter's value chain analysis in Chapter 1, "What Is Cloud Computing?—The Journey to Cloud"—direct and indirect activities, it can be said that there are also *direct* and *indirect metrics*. These are metrics that measure financial gain or loss at limited or no distance from the production function (direct)—such as those used to measure performance of an investment portfolio—and metrics that are one or more steps away from the process of revenue generation (indirect)—such as those used to highlight departmental performance.

Let's start with an overview of indirect metrics that measure general business and IT performance. Then, we move to direct metrics that measure the returns on a given set of investments.

Indirect Metrics

Measuring the value of IT investments, whether those investments are for customer-facing environments or for internal operational systems or business support systems (OSS or BSS), begins with an adherence to a robust total cost of ownership (TCO) methodology.

 Note

Functions not directly related to revenue-generating products or processes can still be considered key performance indicators (KPI) or key success indicators (KSI). KPIs and KSIs are typically numeric in nature and can be a subset of either direct or indirect metrics.

It will soon be evident that many of the indirect metrics (such as availability) will be closely related to revenue-generating functions or can serve well in both a direct and an indirect capacity. It is advisable to ensure that the metrics you use for your cloud computing analysis are aligned with those used by your corporate finance department.

TCO is considered by many to be the most important of all KPIs/KSIs and is often used to baseline the "before" picture in advance of investing in new technologies and solutions.

Total Cost of Ownership

Total cost of ownership (TCO) is simply the sum total of all associated costs relating to the purchase, ownership, usage, and maintenance of a particular product.

As with any consumer product—let's say an automobile—there is the end-user cost or the purchase price, and then there are the costs associated with tires, oil, fuel, batteries, and so on over the useful life of the automobile.

Similarly with investments in IT infrastructure and applications, there are costs associated with ownership that are over and above the initial purchase price. There are costs for hardware and software maintenance (the costs paid to the vendor for ongoing support, bug fixes, upgrades, and case escalations.) There are costs for power to run and cool servers, storage, and network hardware in the data center. There are also the costs associated with internal support and break-fix activities (also known as moves, adds, and changes [MAC]).

Depending on the type of investment, it may be either be expensed or capitalized. Small tools and noncapital expenditures under a certain threshold (usually $3,000–$5,000) are typically expensed and are not depreciated over their useful life. Items such as fiber and copper cables often fall into this category. Larger, more expensive items—such as disk storage, servers, tape libraries, switches, routers, computer room air chillers (CRAC) and so on—are considered fixed assets (FA), and are capitalized, and thus depreciated over their useful life. If an asset is depreciated, the depreciation expense should be included in the TCO analysis.

 Note

Generally Accepted Accounting Principles (GAAP) recognizes multiple methods of depreciation, including straight-line, declining, sum of the years' digits, and double-declining. For the purposes of our examples, we use straight-line depreciation only, purely for ease of use.

Note that in the United States, the Internal Revenue Service is the final authority on threshold values and capitalized assets.[1]

---

1. Internal Revenue Manual 1.35.6, "Property and Equipment Accounting," http://www.irs.gov/irm/part1/irm_01-035-006.html, accessed April 2012.

For a basic example of TCO analysis, let's take a disk storage unit that costs $1,000,000 and has a useful life of three years. Using the straight-line depreciation method, the depreciation charge for this unit would be $333,333.33 per year. Additionally, there is a maintenance contract with the vendor for $100,000 annually. The physical footprint of the device equals four tiles in the data center (which we know from our facilities management firm costs $10,000 a year, including power and cooling charges). Finally, the MAC associated with provisioning storage for our clients requires one full-time equivalent (FTE) storage engineer at $150,000 annually. These values are captured in Table 2-1.

Table 2-1   Annual Total Cost of Ownership for a Single Disk Storage Unit

Item	Annual Charge	Three-Year Charge
Disk storage	$333,333.333	$1,000,000.00
Maintenance	$100,000.00	$300,000.00
Facilities	$10,000.00	$30,000.00
FTE labor	$150,000.00	$450,000.00
Total	$593,333.33	$1,780,000.00

With this basic example, you can see that the TCO is $593,333.33 annually and that the TCO over the lifetime of the product is $1,780,000.00.

For an isolated investment such as the previous example, a TCO analysis can be relatively simple. For an entire data center, server farm, or line of business, however, it can be a decisively more complex undertaking.

 Note

Components inside the data center have disjointed life cycles. The useful lives of servers and storage are not coterminous: We have a gap of roughly 18 months between a server's useful life and the useful life of a disk device. If the useful life of a network device is seven to ten years and the data center housing these devices has a useful life of 25 years, we have an even greater disconnect.

Not only does this scenario make for challenging TCO analyses, but as technologies such as server virtualization increase utilization in the data center, the bullwhip effect becomes more prevalent and more costly (refer to Chapter 1).

TCO analysis can be a time-consuming process. Total costs, however, are a critical component of the IT value equation, and TCO analysis is a critical function of managing performance by the numbers. When TCO analysis is executed well, it can provide a clear picture of the costs associated with IT functions and assets throughout the organization.

To execute a quality TCO analysis, a project team with a dedicated charter and executive sponsorship and oversight might be required. Given the internal costs associated with such an undertaking, it can be tempting to go with an outside consultant.

Many cloud providers will use some form of a TCO analysis to demonstrate the offsets associated with migrating to their cloud platform. It can be beneficial to have at least a rough idea of your TCO, broken out by line of business or by application, before discussing it with a cloud provider or consultant. Be careful to protect your intellectual property, and be explicit about the acceptable future use of your data.

Availability

Perhaps one of the simplest and most universal measurements of IT performance is availability. Availability is critical for the success of a platform, regardless of whether its users are internal or external customers.

Availability, plainly put, is the amount of time a service is accessible or usable in a given time window. For a service that is online 24 hours a day, seven days a week, the hours of availability and corresponding minutes of downtime are shown in Table 2-2.

Table 2-2   Availability in Calendar Hours

Hours per Calendar Year	Availability	Minutes of Downtime
525,600	0.99999	5.256
525,600	0.9999	52.56

Availability is typically referred to in terms of nines, as in "five nines" or "four nines" of availability. Five nines availability equates to 5.256 minutes of downtime per calendar year, while four nines equals 52.56 minutes of downtime per year.

What does this mean in monetary terms? If a revenue-impacting application that processes $1 million of orders an hour is offline for 5.256 minutes, the cost to the business is $87,600.

Poor availability, even for nonrevenue-impacting applications, negatively impacts the business. An application outage not only impacts the users' productivity but also consumes the resources of those who support that application. In addition to the productivity losses incurred, the costs of both the downtime and the subsequent troubleshooting and repair must be considered.

Root cause analysis (RCA) and the resulting "postmortem" work can take hundreds of man-hours to complete. The fully burdened costs of an FTE employee diverted from strategic efforts to focus on RCA must be considered as additional costs incurred by the outage (both in terms of the direct costs and the opportunity cost of time taken away from the strategic effort).

For example, if the same environment has a one-hour outage, the direct cost of the downtime totals $1,000,000 in lost or delayed orders. Additional costs of the outage would also include the total amount of FTE hours (times the fully burdened costs) plus the costs of the hours lost or delayed from more strategic work.

Many platforms have different availability targets based on their application type and customer base. For example, a development environment might not subscribe to a typical 24 by 7 operating window, but instead might base availability on the workweek (for example, 9 a.m. to 5 p.m. Monday through Friday). Conversely, a customer-facing application for downloading music or for personal banking that was only available during the workweek would find a very limited market.

Availability targets for application providers vary and should be expressly outlined in their service-level agreements (SLA).

Time to Market

Time to market (TTM) measures the length of time to implement a new application or go to market with a new service.

TTM is a critical measure of a company's capability to execute. Bringing products to market quickly is the shortest path to revenue generation. For an IT department, a low TTM rating is perhaps the single most important metric highlighting the department's ability to support the business while remaining flexible and agile.

If we think back to our IT supply chain analogy, we remember that the "human factor" associated with IT functions and processes—particularly overprovisioning or hoarding resources—contributes heavily to the bullwhip effect. The bullwhip effect can dramatically increase TTM while simultaneously increasing costs.

Consider a simple application requiring disk storage, network access, and coding to connect to and query a database. If each step in this supply chain (storage, network, application) lengthens the time to market, the overall TTM for that application increases.

As TTM increases, a company is at a distinct disadvantage compared with competitors that have a lower TTM. Not only are the costs increasing along with the delays, but the risk of customer loss also increases.

Broken processes, waste, and inefficiency in the IT supply chain increase TTM and risks the company millions of dollars in opportunity costs alone, if not in pure revenue.

Opportunity Costs

Opportunity costs are simply the costs of decisions. In other words, with limited or scarce resources, an investment in Project 1 prohibits investment in Project 2. If Project 2 nets a return of $1,000 and Project 1 nets a zero-dollar return, the opportunity cost of choosing Project 1 (and not choosing Project 2) is $1,000.

 Note

Contrast *opportunity costs* with *sunk costs*. Sunk costs are the costs associated with investments that have already been made. In our earlier examples, sunk costs are a function of previous investments in hardware, software, and time that will not be recouped except through their continued use. It is typically advised that sunk costs be excluded from the decision-making process for new investments for the precise reason that no matter what you do, you will not get that money back. Additionally, sunk costs have already been recorded and factored into previous reporting cycles. Sunk costs should especially be excluded from decisions regarding new platforms that have the ability to increase growth or prohibit customer churn.

Churn Rate

A critical measure of a company's overall performance is its *churn rate*. A company's churn rate indicates how many customers have been lost within a given time period (typically monthly, quarterly, or annually). As you have probably guessed, the customer churn rate is essentially the opposite of the company's customer growth rate, or how many customers have been added during that same window of time.

Churn can be considered a *key performance indicator (KPI)*, and use of indirect metrics can help mitigate the rate of churn. Poor availability of services can contribute heavily to a company's churn rate. A severe prolonged outage can cost a company hundreds if not thousands of customers overnight. In a highly competitive vertical—such as wireless and mobile communications—a customer you lose is a customer *your competitor* gains.

Other indirect metrics, such as TTM, can contribute heavily to a company's churn rate. If a service provider is consistently late to market with new products, it will lose customers to its competitors that have the ability to execute quickly and can go to market swiftly with new offerings.

Productivity

A simple measure of the effectiveness of a department or company is *productivity*. Productivity can be measured in a number of ways (units produced per hour, cases closed per month, and so on). At a macro level, however, this metric can be calculated as total revenues per headcount.

A company with 50 employees and revenues of $500,000 annually has a (revenue) productivity rate of $10,000 per headcount.

Revenue per headcount (or employee revenue productivity) is perhaps the highest-level metric, providing executives with visibility to aggregate corporate performance. While the benefits of this metric are its simplicity and ease of use, the downsides should be obvious: Any department outside of sales might find difficulty aligning its performance to this number.

Other Metrics

As a rule, business performance in aggregate is much easier to measure than the value of a single process inside a business. Certain processes inherently map more cleanly than others to traditional measures of value.

Business units responsible for building products for sale to market are typically measured on revenues, market share, and units sold. Expenses are often measured as well to ensure that the business unit's profitability is in line with the company's overall targets. This is a relatively straightforward proposition.

Nonfinancial metrics or other measures of success can be included in the mutually accepted goals of the organization—perhaps as a part of a team's Vision, Strategy, and Execution (VSE).

Often, IT functions are not directly tied to the revenue of the company, so many departments or application owners use nonfinancial KPIs or KSIs to guide, measure, and report performance.

 Note

> Notable exceptions might include supply chain management (SCM) functions that determine how much raw materials to purchase for assembly of products, or customer relationship management (CRM) tools responsible for direct customer interaction.
>
> Other exceptions to this rule could include applications related to sales commissions, order entry, and accounts payable. Even still, these applications are often one or two steps removed from the revenue-generating process. In other words, a business could still generate revenue without them—albeit much less effectively—in a worst-case scenario.

Vision, Strategy, and Execution

A Vision, Strategy, and Execution (VSE) template is a good place to compile nonfinancial KPIs for a team or a department. A stripped-down VSE from a VP of application architecture might look something like the example in Table 2-3.

Table 2-3   Vision, Strategy, and Execution

Category	Description
Vision	Design and build the next-generation business platforms required to enable our company's market success.
Strategy	Integrate core application functionality with best-of-breed technologies.
Execution	Align critical resources to growth areas. Upgrade and migrate the application portal.

Obviously, this is just a simple example, but you should be able to get a feel from this exercise for how a VSE can help guide an organization's performance. A fully fleshed-out VSE would have a more detailed vision statement and possibly four or five accompanying strategy and execution elements.

Using Table 2-3, we can demonstrate how KPIs can be rolled up as supporting documentation. In a more detailed plan, KPIs such as the numbers of application failures or the numbers of cases related to application access could be used to register a baseline for a before-and-after measurement.

To continue with this exercise, an example of a baseline KPI might be the number of IT support cases related to application access issues: poor application performance over the WAN, users unable to load the application landing screen, failed logins, and so on.

For the sake of argument, let's say that the high-water mark for this KPI (application access) was 1,000 cases last fiscal year. As a part of this executive's strategy element, "Integrate core application functionality with best-of-breed technologies," she intends to "upgrade and migrate the application portal" (execution element). At the end of the following fiscal year, this KPI will hopefully have decreased dramatically. Subsequently, the reduction in this KPI should enable her to also "align critical resources to growth areas."

Just as the execution components of this VSE comprise the strategy, this VP's VSE should be part of the CIO's overarching VSE, at least to some degree. The CIO's VSE should also include representation from security, finance IT, manufacturing IT, and so on. Having all of these VSEs integrated at some level in the CIO's overall strategy demonstrates strong functional alignment and cohesive planning.

Note

Customer satisfaction (CSAT) is a KPI used both externally (to measure the satisfaction of paying customers) and internally (any employee who uses an IT service is a customer of IT). Typically, CSAT is measured through surveys and interviews, with resulting answers tied to a numeric value. In the previous example, a high number of failed logins would negatively impact CSAT for this organization. Mean time to repair (MTTR) and other metrics—like service-level agreement (SLA) performance—are often a subset of CSAT.

Service-Level Agreements

Service-level agreements (SLA) are tools commonly used to establish mutual expectations between providers and consumers of services. SLA performance is a highly useful KPI. A typical SLA will include an outline of service availability (five nines, for example—99.999 percent availability) with an expectation of some sort of remuneration if the SLA is missed. If remuneration is not outlined in the SLA, the agreement is said to "lack teeth."

It is important to note that most public cloud providers do offer some type of SLA. For example, the SLA for the Google Apps service outlines Google's refund policy (days of service credited to the consumer) based on service availability.[2] Amazon's EC2 SLA outlines a target of 99.5 percent availability during a service year.[3]

Quality Initiatives

Quality initiatives such as Kaizen, Total Quality Management (TQM), or Six Sigma utilize KPIs as benchmarks for critical processes and as starting points for increasing the performance of a department or a function.

Six Sigma, for example, is a well-established quality initiative that includes the DMAIC methodology (define, measure, analyze, improve, control) for process improvement and control. The term *Six Sigma* comes from statistics: A process that shows a variation of six sigma—six standard deviations from the mean—shows a deviation of no more than 3.4 defects per million.[4] Six Sigma, and in particular DMAIC, are especially useful in resolving broken or poor-performing IT processes.

2. Google, Inc. Google Apps Service Level Agreement, www.google.com/apps/intl/en/terms/sla.html, accessed December 2011.

3. Amazon's EC2 Service Level Agreement, http://aws.amazon.com/ec2-sla/, accessed January 2012.

4. Ho, Lin C. "How to Apply 6 Sigma Quality Practices to Your Business," E-Week.com, www.eweek.com/c/a/IT-Management/How-to-Apply-Six-Sigma-Quality-Practices-to-Your-Business/, accessed December 2011.

Let's use a concrete example: IT storage and administration. Storage is a critical function of the IT supply chain. Without storage processes and controls, applications cannot run. Therefore, one KPI for an IT storage support team might be mean time to repair (MTTR) for fulfillment of new storage requests. Another KPI for the same team might be the numbers of cases closed in a given amount of time (for example, monthly or quarterly).

If the average time to close a case for adding and masking new logical unit numbers (LUN) is one week, a quality initiative for the storage organization could be the reduction of the overall MTTR to three days or less. The DMAIC process could be used to determine which processes, as a part of the LUN assignment function, are perhaps highly susceptible to human error. As a part of this overall quality initiative, the team could look to automate or even eliminate functions that repeatedly cause errors or create rework.

Another quality initiative might be to reduce the numbers of storage cases opened by improving the capacity-planning process further upstream. Six Sigma processes, including DMAIC, could be applied to a wider set of problem statements—application growth, budget appropriation, purchasing—to enhance overall customer satisfaction in the application user base by reducing downtime and increasing the speed of upgrades (measured in MTTR).

Implementing quality initiatives can be time-consuming and—for complex, multifaceted problems—can take months or even years to demonstrate significant results. A Six Sigma project requires a certain level of expertise and corporate knowledge, which can necessitate the reallocation of expert resources from other ongoing engagements. Therefore, to ensure success, a Six Sigma effort (or any other prolonged quality initiative) requires senior-level executive sponsorship and tight alignment with the priorities of the business.

 Note

The cost of poor quality (COPQ) is a quality measurement that refers broadly to the delta between a customer's expectations of a product (or service) and its actual performance. With respect to IT and IT infrastructure, COPQ can be used to measure the costs associated with poor utilization. Poor utilization of IT assets (CPU, storage, and network) stems from many structural and functional sources. Inadequate capacity planning (coupled with "siloed" business functions) is often the most frequent source of poor utilization.

If a customer purchases $1 million worth of servers and only uses 10 percent of the CPU capacity, the waste factor or COPQ is $900,000. Obviously, the COPQ associated with poor utilization can equate to multiple millions of dollars lost annually.

At this point, we have discussed a number of indirect metrics used to measure the business impact of IT functions not directly related to revenue generation.

An essential part of moving IT from a cost center to a strategic asset is measuring the value that is created by core IT processes and functions, and then structuring your initiatives to take advantage of that value elsewhere in IT or in other parts of the business.

It is critical to understand that consumption of cloud resources does not directly equate to abandoning core IT processes and functions. While there is a high likelihood that utilizing resources in the cloud will materially affect processes and functions currently in place, we are primarily concerned with demonstrating the value creation and cost reductions associated with moving specific functions into the cloud.

As you justify a migration to the cloud, it might also be worthwhile to measure and demonstrate the value of those functions that are likely to remain unchanged as a part of this migration. This information could prove immensely valuable and enable you to uncover untapped strategic resources in your business.

Now that we have discussed *indirect metrics*, let us shift our focus to *direct metrics* and measuring the impact of investments directly related to the revenue-generating functions of the company.

Direct Metrics

The list of meaningful and relevant financial metrics is long, and to cover each of them here in detail would be a time-consuming (if not overwhelming) proposition.

For our purposes, we cover the metrics most frequently used to guide and report business performance. As you apply the measurement and valuation processes to your own environment, be certain to use the same metrics and guidelines used by your chief financial officer (CFO), program management office (PMO), or other governing body inside your company. This will ensure that the value is measured in the same fashion and that the resulting data will be meaningful to senior executives.

In the following sections, we look closely at the most common direct or financial metrics used to measure corporate and investment performance. These include

- Payback method
- Net present value (NPV)
- Return on investment (ROI)
- Economic value added (EVA)
- Return on assets (ROA)
- Return on equity (ROE)

Payback Method

The payback method is a relatively "quick and dirty" method of evaluating investment performance. Its popularity stems primarily from its ease of use. The payback method simply measures the length of time required to recoup the investment in a product or service. A product that allows the purchaser to recoup his or her investment quickly is deemed a better investment than one that has a lengthy payback period.

Here is a simple example: An investment in new high-performance server technology enables the customer to process orders twice as quickly as the old system. On average, the old system processed $100,000 of orders every two months. The new system, which costs $50,000, processes the same amount of orders in one month. In this example, the investment in new servers reaches its payback amount in the first two weeks of the first month (estimate an average of $25,000 of orders per week).

The payback method is certainly simple—it does not require a spreadsheet and can be done in your head or on a cocktail napkin. The payback method does, however, have its faults. Primarily, the payback method does not take into account the time value of money (TVM), which is considered critical for large investments or investments whose benefits extend over longer periods of time.

The lack of a time function means that the payback method is not equipped to handle many of the variables associated with large investments over several years (for example, real estate for a new data center or the construction of a new data center facility). Enter net present value (NPV).

Net Present Value

NPV analysis has the facility to account for both the time value of money (TVM) and—through the use of a *discount rate*—either a company's weighted average cost of capital (WACC) or a predetermined *hurdle rate*. Let's discuss each of these concepts in more detail.

TVM is the principle that money has the potential to increase in value over time—the opportunity to invest means the potential to create value. The rate used to determine how much a dollar invested earns or creates can be an interest rate, such as that offered by a bank on interest-bearing accounts. A *discount rate* is used to determine the *present value* of an investment (you might think of this as the inverse of compounding interest). For the purposes of NPV analysis, the discount rate will likely either be the company's predetermined *hurdle rate* or the company's *weighted average cost of capital (WACC)*.

Note

A *hurdle rate* is typically predetermined by the finance department or the PMO to set a gate for capital investments. An investment with a projected return lower than the prescribed hurdle rate should not receive funding. Using the hurdle rate as the rate in an NPV calculation ensures that a project with a positive NPV is aligned with the company's overall investment guidelines.

There has been so much research and study on the weighted average cost of capital (WACC) that it is hard to do the concept justice here. At the risk of oversimplification, a company's cost of capital is the market value of its overall financial structure. WACC is a measure of the cost of a company's equity and the cost of its debt after taxes.

As stated previously, NPV calculations require a discount rate for measurement. It is recommended that you use a prescribed hurdle rate or your company's WACC to ensure tight alignment with corporate finance and the company's overall investment guidelines.

The *future value* of an investment is assumed to be larger at the end of a period of time because of the discount rate. Conversely, the *present value* of an investment today is less than it will be at a predetermined point in the future.[5]

For example, with an interest rate of 5 percent, the *future value* of one dollar in one year is $1.05 [$1 + (.05 * $1.00)]. See Table 2-4.

Conversely, the *present value* of one dollar one year from now with a discount rate of 5 percent is $0.9523 ($1.00/1.05). See Table 2-4.

Table 2-4   Present and Future Value of One Dollar at 5 Percent Interest for One Year

Present Value of Future $1	Value of $1 at Present	Future Value of Present $1
$0.9523	$1.00	$1.05

The NPV of an investment is the present value of all future benefits (cash flows, savings, offsets, deferrals, and so on) generated by that investment, discounted over set intervals of time, and net of any initial startup costs or investments.

---

5. Stephen A. Ross, Randolph W. Westerfield, and Jeffrey Jaffe, *Corporate Finance*, Fifth Edition. Irwin/McGraw-Hill, 1999, p. 65.

NPV analysis is frequently used to justify investments and capital expenditures. The benefits of using NPV analysis are the relative precision of the results (stemming from the use of TVM) and the simplicity of the decision-making process: A positive NPV indicates a good investment.

Finally, opportunity costs are accounted for implicitly with the use of a discount rate (whether it is the WACC or the hurdle rate): If a projected rate of return is less than the company's desired rate of return, it is best that the funding for that investment is kept on the sidelines.

For companies investing in new business models, NPV analysis allows managers and decision makers to estimate the value of new cash flows with respect to the company's capital structure. Knowledge of NPV principles allows managers to make decisions based on the timing of positive inflows.

For companies evaluating capital investments or making "build or buy" decisions— for example, building private clouds versus leveraging public cloud resources—NPV analysis allows decision makers to choose an investment that meets a company's cost-of-capital restrictions.

Example of Net Present Value

In the next chapter, we use NPV to measure the benefits of investing in a cloud computing solution, but first let's start with a simple example to ensure that we understand the math behind NPV.

Using a rate of return of 10 percent, what is the NPV of a $1 million investment with cash inflows of $500,000 each year for three years?

This is calculated as follows:

NPV = –$1,000,000 + [$500,000/(1.1)] + [$500,000/(1.1^2)] + [$500,000/(1.1^3)]

NPV = –$1,000,000 + $454,545.45 + $413,223.14 + $375,657.40

NPV = $243,426.00

The result is a positive NPV of $243,426, indicating that this is a good investment. Note: The annual cash inflows are discounted by the rate each year (10 percent in year 1, 10 percent squared in year 2, and 10 percent cubed in year 3). The NPV function in Microsoft Excel does this for you behind the scenes.

Note

A Google search of *NPV Excel is wrong* will return a number of links claiming that Microsoft Excel calculates NPV incorrectly. This is not exactly the case.

By default, Excel assumes that the initial payment occurs at the end of the first period. Therefore, Excel will discount the initial outflow if it is included in the formula. If the payment is at the beginning of the first period, you must subtract the initial outflow as a last step to avoid having it discounted.

If the payment occurs at the beginning of period 1, the same calculation in Excel is handled as follows:

=NPV(rate, cash inflow year 1, cash inflow year 2, cash inflow year 3, . . .) – Initial outflow

=NPV(.10, 500000, 500000, 500000) – $1000000

= $1,243,426 – $1,000,000

= $243,426.00

If the initial payment is at the end of the first period, the NPV function in Excel can be used without the last step shown here.[6]

Return on Investment

Return on investment (ROI), is possibly the most common tool used to justify (or deny) capital investments for IT. ROI calculators can be found for nearly every IT spending category. ROI is relatively straightforward to use—and (unfortunately) misuse.

The formula for ROI is simple:

ROI = (Gains from investment – Costs of investment) / (Costs of investment)

Here is an example of ROI using the same numbers from our previous NPV example:

ROI = ($1,500,000 – $1,000,000) / $1,000,000

ROI = 50%

---

6. Microsoft Office Help, "NPV," http://office.microsoft.com/en-us/sharepoint-foundation-help/npv-function-HA010380009.aspx?CTT=1, accessed January 2012.

Unadjusted ROI assumes the present value for all gains and costs (that is, all costs and returns are immediate). Hence, using ROI without adjusting for the time value of money can be problematic when measuring returns over long periods of time.

Given that a simple ROI calculation does not account for TVM, the periods of gains can be extended as needed to increase the ROI. This is the most common example of ROI misuse.

It is possible to fine-tune ROI calculations (and payback calculations for that matter) by using present value discounting in conjunction with traditional methods of calculation.

For example (using the same numbers as shown previously):

ROI = (Present value of all gains – All costs) / (All costs)

ROI = [($454,545.45 + $413,223.14 + $375,657.40) – $1,000,000] / $1,000,000

ROI = 24.343%

The ROI, when discounted for present value (in other words, when adjusted for the time value of money), is significantly less than the unadjusted ROI. However, if the resulting ROI is higher than the company's hurdle rate, this would still be a good investment.

Whenever possible, it is a good practice to use present value–discounted metrics.

Other Direct Metrics

Up to this point, we have outlined the three most common metrics used to measure project-based success (payback, ROI, and NPV). To separate these metrics from quality-driven metrics and programs (like KPIs and Six Sigma), we have labeled these as *direct metrics*. There are other direct metrics you should be aware of, such as economic value added (EVA), return on assets (ROA), and return on equity (ROE).

While these metrics can be used with a single line of business or a single project, use of these metrics in this fashion can be problematic. The primary issue with such usage models is that these metrics typically account for the firm's tax rate.

EVA—a method devised by Stern Stewart and Company for measuring value creation—is calculated as follows:

EVA = Net operating profit after taxes (NOPAT) – (Capital * Cost of capital)

This formula can be adjusted and applied to a single line of business or investment by changing NOPAT to net benefits:

EVA = Net benefits – (Capital * Cost of capital)

In this case, the net benefits of a project are matched to the capital responsible for the benefits, and the company's cost of capital is accounted for. This is a perfectly legitimate use of EVA as long as net benefits and capital are cleanly mapped and the changes are clearly noted.

ROA and ROE, however, are less easily modified in that they are more comprehensive and include the company's debt and tax burden. ROE, for example, measures returns against a company's shareholder equity, making it virtually impossible to apply to a single project or product. ROA typically measures net income after taxes against a company's asset base, again making it quite difficult to isolate against a single investment.

Conclusion

In this chapter, we established the notion of *direct* and *indirect metrics*. Direct metrics can be used to measure the financial impact of a single project or line of business contributing directly to the revenue-generation process. Indirect metrics, on the other hand, can measure departmental performance one or two levels removed from revenue generation.

Quality-based initiatives, such as Six Sigma, are often used to drive process improvements across departments or even across entire corporations. These initiatives, while increasing customer satisfaction, might not necessarily contribute directly to the firm's bottom line.

Direct metrics, such as the payback method, return on investment, and net present value, can be used to measure project-based performance (such as investment in new data center infrastructure). Other direct metrics (such as return on assets and return on equity) are typically used to measure overall corporate financial performance.

In the next chapter, we apply payback method, ROI, and NPV to examples of cloud computing investments to simplify the process of justifying the migration to cloud platforms.

3

Sample Case Studies— Applied Metrics

In this chapter, we review the three most common direct metrics (net present value, return on investment, and payback), and apply each metric to three examples of investments in cloud computing and service models:

- *Software licensing: Software as a Service (SaaS)*

- *Disaster recovery and high availability: Infrastructure as a Service (IaaS)*

- *New application development and deployment: Platform as a Service (PaaS)*

To establish a working baseline for each of these scenarios, we first need to establish the total cost of ownership (TCO).

Total Cost of Ownership

As we saw in the previous chapter, understanding the TCO of a solution or an environment is a critical precedent for measuring improvements in cost structures in an IT value chain.

George Reese, in his book *Cloud Application Architectures* (O'Reilly, 2009), outlines the importance of measuring the TCO of the "before" picture.[1] As we have stated, it is critical to understand the current usage models before implementing a cloud-based solution. After the baseline usage and costs have been established, calculating the benefits of a move to the cloud becomes relatively academic.

Reese puts together a clear and succinct model for understanding the costs associated with a move to the cloud (versus the current costs of legacy environments). Reese argues that if your usage patterns are relatively static, your savings in the cloud will be nominal (or potentially even nonexistent). On the other hand, if your consumption varies widely above or below planned capacity on an ongoing basis, your savings will be much higher.[2]

Application usage measured independently of the overall infrastructure can be misleading. It is critical to understand the total consumption at a departmental or corporate level to determine true costs as well as true savings.

Building on our previous examples, we can create a TCO for a typical IT department (or, in keeping with our analogy, a typical IT supply chain). With this baseline in place, we will be able to layer on top our use cases (software licensing, disaster recovery/high availability, and new application deployment) for comparison purposes. After we have established the before and after picture, we can use our direct metrics to outline our cost savings and financial benefits.

For our examples throughout this chapter, we use Omicron, Inc., a fictional biotechnology company with a proven track record of helping its customers reduce their time to market for new drugs. Omicron began life as a research firm processing large clinical data sets for companies like Wyeth and Eli Lilly. With the addition of new partners, Omicron began adding research and development as well as marketing and branding services.

Omicron is now a full-service clinical research organization with an employee base of 100 individuals (including IT, sales, research, and design) operating out of Palo Alto, California. Omicron has a small data center today where it hosts its customer databases, research libraries, and sales and finance applications.

---

1. George Reese. *Cloud Application Architectures*. Sebastapol, CA: O'Reilly Media, Inc. 2009, pp. 52–53.

2. Ibid. p. 53.

Omicron has signed two major contracts in the past three years, contributing to 100 percent revenue growth year over year. The company currently hosts customer data in excess of 500 TB, supported by a relatively small IT staff of 20 engineers and developers. Traffic on Omicron's online portal (where the company shares data with development teams at partner firms) has grown 60 percent in the last two quarters.

In Table 3-1, I have used our original storage example (shown previously in Table 2-1), but I have doubled the capacity and (accordingly) the facilities footprint. In addition, I have increased the facilities charge to include the server real estate as well.

Table 3-1   Annual Total Cost of Ownership for Omicron's IT Supply Chain

Item	Annual Charge	Three-Year Charge
Disk storage	$666,666.67	$2,000,000.00
Disk maintenance	$100,000.00	$300,000.00
Facilities	$30,000.00	$90,000.00
Full-time equivalent (FTE) labor	$900,000.00	$2,700,000.00
Firewalls and load balancers	$10,000.00	$30,000.00
Network switches	$10,000.00	$30,000.00
Server hardware	$166,666.67	$500,000.00
Server maintenance	$20,000.00	$60,000.00
Software licenses	$66,666.67	$200,000.00
Total	**$1,970,000.01**	**$5,910,000.00**

To account for the servers and applications, I have added server hardware and maintenance and customer relationship management (CRM) software licenses. I have also included basic switching, routing, and load-balancing hardware for network access. Finally, I have increased the engineering FTE charges—six individuals at $150,000 per year—to cover administration of the storage, network, server, and software platforms.

The total annual run rate is $1.97 million (and one penny) for the depreciation of all hardware and software (using straight-line depreciation over three years) and for facilities and labor expenses. Omicron's total cost of ownership over three years is $5.91 million.

These are rough estimates for a relatively small IT environment. As always, costs for items such as electricity and labor vary by geography. Customer purchasing power also plays a role: Customers with larger budgets are often able to negotiate better discounts. Therefore, costs associated with typical IT resources in one scenario can differ greatly from those in another seemingly similar scenario.

With Omicron's TCO baseline now established, we can examine the financial impact—using direct metrics—of implementing each of the three cloud computing service models.

Software Licensing: SaaS

To support its growing customer base and to help meet its forecasted revenue targets, three years ago Omicron invested in a complex CRM software package for tracking customer opportunities and contacts. Omicron senior management had hoped the CRM package would enable its sales force to be more productive; however, the package it selected was cumbersome and difficult to maintain. Upgrades to enable specific features and functionality required extensive system customization and frequent, lengthy outages.

Based on their research, the IT and Sales leadership teams at Omicron now believe they should move their CRM instance to a cloud-based platform. Depending on the outcome of financial what-if scenarios, they might move to a per-seat license model for a new Software as a Service CRM solution.

TCO with Software as a Service

Table 3-2 highlights the changes to Omicron's existing TCO model.

Table 3-2 Annual Total Cost of Ownership for Omicron's IT Supply Chain (SaaS)		
Item	**Annual Charge**	**Three-Year Charge**
Disk storage	$333,333.33	$1,000,000.00
Disk maintenance	$50,000.00	$150,000.00
Facilities	$15,000.00	$45,000.00
Full-time equivalent (FTE) labor	$900,000.00	$2,700,000.00
Firewalls and load balancers	$10,000.00	$30,000.00
Network switches	$10,000.00	$30,000.00

Item	Annual Charge	Three-Year Charge
Server hardware	$83,333.33	$250,000.00
Server maintenance	$10,000.00	$30,000.00
Software licenses	$70,833.33	$212,500.00
Total	**$1,482,499.99**	**$4,447,500.00**

We have reduced the storage footprint by half. In this model, we are only removing the CRM package from the customer premises. The remaining applications (payroll, email, and so on) will stay put. Consequently, we have reduced the storage maintenance, server hardware and maintenance, and facilities charges by half.

FTE labor for now stays the same—we are not reducing IT headcount as a result of this move.

The software license charge for this example has increased slightly to $212,500. This is our initial outflow or investment. The assumption here is that Omicron has purchased a yearly license with enough headroom to cover new employees as they are added.

Again, these are variables that can be adjusted as necessary to reflect market-specific data.

Software as a Service Cost Comparison

In Table 3-3, we show the savings Omicron can achieve by moving from the legacy model to the SaaS model. In the legacy model, Omicron spends $1.88 million annually—a three-year cost of $5.64 million. After moving to a Software as a Service platform, Omicron spends $1.4375 million annually, or $4.3125 million over three years. On the surface, this appears to be a good investment. To ensure that this is a sound use of finances, the resulting annual savings ($442,500.01) can be positioned against the costs and analyzed through our payback, NPV, and ROI models.

Table 3-3   Software as a Service Cost Comparison

Item	Annual Cost/Savings	Three-Year Charge
Legacy-model TCO	$1,970,000.01	$5,910,000.00
SaaS-model TCO	$1,482,499.99	$4,447,500.00
Savings	$487,500.02	$1,462,500.00

Using the payback method with $212,500 as our initial investment (our cost for the new licenses) and $$487,500.02 as our return (reducing the amount of on-premise storage and related facilities charges), Omicron reaches payback in just less than six months:

$212,500 / $487,500.02 = 0.43

0.43 * 12 months = 5.23 months

A documented payback on a cloud investment in less than one year is respectable. Depending on Omicron's performance metrics (its KPIs and KSIs), however, this might or might not be a good investment. Let's assume that Omicron is looking for a payback on this project in less than a year. It is still important to measure the investment performance using not only payback but also ROI and NPV.

Recall that our formula for ROI is simply the gains from the investment minus the costs of the investment divided by the costs of the investment. In this case:

ROI = (Gains from investment – Costs of investment) / (Costs of investment)

ROI = ($487,500.02 – $212,500.00) / $212,500.00

ROI = 129.41%

A one-year ROI of 129 percent is substantial to be sure; however, here we are still not taking into account the time value of money.[3] By simply using ROI and payback, we are ignoring the longer-term value—and potentially the longer-term risk—of the investment. Therefore, let's consider the impact of this investment over the course of three years, using net present value analysis.

Net present value analysis, as demonstrated in the previous chapter, uses a discount rate, which can be a hurdle rate or the company's weighted average cost of capital, alongside the cash outflows and inflows starting in the first year.

In Omicron's SaaS example, the NPV is calculated as follows (using a discount rate of 10 percent):

NPV = –$212,500 + ($487,500.02/1.1) + [$487,500.02/(1.1^2)] + [$487,500.02/(1.1^3)]

NPV = –$212,500 + $443,181.84 + $402,892.58 + $366,265.98

NPV = $999,840.40

---

3. The three-year ROI—not discounted for TVM—would be the same given that the subscription price for the SaaS licensing is an annual cost.

In this case, the three-year NPV of moving to an SaaS framework for Omicron's CRM application is $999,840.40. As we established in the previous chapter, a positive NPV indicates a good investment. All three direct metrics indicate that implementing a SaaS strategy is a good use of the company's funds. Of the three direct metrics, NPV gives us the most comprehensive view, taking into account the longer-term risks and benefits of this investment using the time value of money.

 Note

Internal rate of return (IRR) can be used with net present value (NPV) analysis. A manual calculation of IRR is an iterative process whereby the user determines the rate required for NPV to equal zero. If the IRR is greater than the discount rate (the hurdle rate or the WAAC) used in the NPV analysis, the project is a good investment.[4]

If you think about it, this is completely logical. We have already determined that a negative NPV is a bad investment and a positive NPV is a good investment. If the IRR is the rate that makes NPV equal to zero, when the IRR is higher than the rate, the NPV will be positive.

To avoid the trial-and-error process associated with manually calculating IRR, Microsoft Excel can be used.

In Excel the formula is

    =IRR(values, guess)

where the values are the cash flows associated with the project in a selected range (for example, A1:A3) and guess is your guess at the rate. If a guess is omitted, 10 percent is used by default.[5]

Table 3-4 summarizes the results of our analysis on the SaaS CRM upgrade.

Table 3-4   Software as a Service Analysis Summary

Method	Payback	ROI	NPV
Value	5.23 months	129.41%	$999,840.40

---

4. Stephen A. Ross, Randolph W. Westerfield, Jeffrey Jaffe, *Corporate Finance*, Fifth Edition. Irwin/McGraw-Hill, 1999, pp. 140–141.

5. Microsoft Office Help, "IRR," http://office.microsoft.com/en-us/excel-help/ irr-HP005209146.aspx, accessed December 2011.

Our analysis shows that Omicron's selection of an SaaS provider for its CRM platform is beneficial to the company over the long term. The reduction in customer premises hardware and the associated facilities and maintenance costs are significant enough on an annual basis—even without a reduction in headcount—to justify the costs of investing in a SaaS solution.

 Note

> Even if Omicron's investment in an SaaS-based CRM package were five times as expensive—$1,062,500.00—the NPV would still be positive: $149,840.40. The three-year ROI—adjusted for TVM—in that case would be 14.1%.

Let's now turn to the next use case to determine the financial impact of investing in cloud computing for disaster recovery and high availability.

Disaster Recovery and Business Continuity: IaaS

As Omicron continues to grow its customer base, its data requirements will continue to grow accordingly. A 30 percent corporate growth rate establishes a low watermark for data growth. As the number of Omicron's customers and partners increases, the amount of data Omicron needs to manage and analyze—not only for business intelligence purposes but also for compliance and disaster recovery—increases dramatically.

It is not uncommon to have four or more copies of every record in a database stored across multiple databases supporting production environments as well as test, development, and quality assurance (QA) efforts. For Omicron to be successful in its marketing initiatives, IT will need to roll out new applications that analyze and take advantage of valuable customer data. That analysis cannot be done on live, production records without the risk of performance degradation or even worse: data loss.

If Omicron intends to be competitive in the marketplace—to prevent unplanned downtime involving the costly loss of customer data and potentially permanent destruction of its own intellectual property—it will need to have a comprehensive long-term business continuity and disaster recovery strategy.

As stated earlier, Omicron has a thriving enterprise in Palo Alto, and its data is growing at a minimum of 30 percent annually. In its current mode of growth, however, the company has not yet established a disaster recovery (DR) or business continuity (BC) plan. Senior management has determined that they cannot afford a critical outage and has mandated that DR and BC are a priority for this fiscal year.

Given Omicron's current lack of DR infrastructure, management has determined that a single application outage could cost Omicron in excess of half a million dollars in revenue. Indeed, its analysis has shown that a five-hour outage because of data loss would not only incur the loss of $500,000 in revenue but also would cost numerous man-hours for troubleshooting and repair.

Omicron has evaluated several options including leasing data center space in northern Washington for failover purposes. The costs associated with the lease and the required facilities, coupled with the costs of owning and managing redundant servers, however, were prohibitive. To provide fully redundant systems in Bellingham that corresponded like for like to the production systems in Palo Alto, Omicron estimated it would face an incremental cost of over $1 million annually. The costs associated with like-for-like failover environments are shown in Table 3-5.

Table 3-5   Like-for-Like Disaster Recovery Cost Summary

Item	Annual Charge	Three-Year Charge
Disk storage	$666,666.67	$2,000,000.00
Disk maintenance	$100,000.00	$300,000.00
Facilities	$30,000.00	$90,000.00
Firewalls and load balancers	$10,000.00	$30,000.00
Network switches	$10,000.00	$30,000.00
Server hardware	$166,666.67	$500,000.00
Server maintenance	$20,000.00	$60,000.00
Software licenses	$66,666.67	$200,000.00
Total	$1,070,000.01	$3,210,000.00

The costs associated with the redundant systems in Washington are essentially the same as the costs for the operation in Palo Alto minus the additional labor. Economies of scale are at work here given that the DR systems in Washington can be managed remotely, save for items requiring on-premise labor such as installing or tracing cables.

These costs do not include the additional overhead associated with replicating the environments from Palo Alto to Bellingham. Automating new processes like copying transaction logs and testing disaster recovery functionality will require significant man-hour investments. For now, however, assume that those costs will be subsumed in the annual FTE costs.

Cost-Benefit Analysis for Server Virtualization

Given the operational costs associated with creating fully redundant systems in Bellingham, the management team is also evaluating server virtualization as part of their DR strategy. While migrating to a virtualized platform such as VMware VSphere 5 or Microsoft Hyper-V will also require significant process overhaul—perhaps even a complete rebuild of the company's IT supply chain—the benefits of virtualization over time (such as reducing the physical server footprint and increasing the utilization of the infrastructure) could be impactful.

Omicron's nonvirtualized server infrastructure costs are highlighted in Table 3-6.

Table 3-6 Nonvirtualized Server Cost Summary Excluding FTE Costs		
Item	Annual Charge	Three-Year Charge
Facilities	$15,000.00	$45,000.00
Server hardware	$166,666.67	$500,000.00
Server maintenance	$20,000.00	$60,000.00
Software licenses	$66,666.67	$200,000.00
Total	$268,333.34	$805,000.00

Here, I have decreased by half the facilities costs to focus only on server consumption. I have included the remaining server costs for a baseline of $268,333.34 annually (or $805,000.00 total over the course of three years).

The capacity-planning team believes that the current utilization rate on the server infrastructure is below 20 percent on an annual average basis. At peak load—immediately after customer acquisition, for example—system utilization approaches 65 percent, but during the rest of the year, the systems remain nearly idle.

Using a 4:1 virtualization ratio (four virtual servers to one physical server, or V-to-P) as a target, the capacity-planning team believes they can reclaim significant savings in infrastructure costs after an investment in licenses for hypervisor software. Furthermore, the leadership team believes that an investment in virtualization not only will save them infrastructure costs but will also help enable their disaster recovery strategy.

Table 3-7 shows the costs associated with the virtualized infrastructure.

Table 3-7   Virtualized Server Cost Summary Excluding FTE Costs

Item	Annual Charge	Three-Year Charge
Hypervisor licenses	$41,666.67	$125,000.00
Facilities	$3,750.00	$11,250.00
Server hardware	$41,666.67	$125,000.00
Server maintenance	$5,000.00	$15,000.00
Software licenses	$16,666.67	$50,000.00
Total	**$108,750.00**	**$326,250.01**

Anticipating Omicron's continued growth, we have included $125,000 for hypervisor licensing depreciated over three years. Using the 4:1 V-to-P ratio as a target, the remaining server-related charges from Table 3-6—facilities, hardware, maintenance, and other software licenses—are divided by 4.

Sizable FTE gains can result from reducing the physical server footprint by 75 percent. The number of hours required for troubleshooting cable problems, configuration issues, security holes, and so on could be one-quarter of the current total. Additionally, there are downstream benefits associated with increasing hardware utilization across the entire infrastructure. Sub-20 percent utilization on the server platform could equate to sub-20 percent utilization on the network. Looked at another way, this would equate to an 80 percent waste factor: 80 cents of every server and network dollar spent could be considered "stranded" or wasted.

For the purposes of this discussion, however, we look strictly at the benefits of reducing hardware and software costs. The comparison of the nonvirtualized and virtualized costs is shown in Table 3-8.

Table 3-8   Summary Comparison of Nonvirtualized and Virtualized Costs

Item	Annual Charge/Savings	Three-Year Charge/ Savings
Nonvirtualized	$268,333.34	$805,000.00
Virtualized	$108,750.00	$326,250.01
Total savings	**$159,583.34**	**$478,750.00**

Looking strictly at server costs (excluding FTE charges, utilization rates, and so on), Omicron can invest $125,000 over three years to consolidate its server footprint by a 4-to-1 ratio. In turn, Omicron will save nearly $160,000 annually.

A quick analysis indicates a 27.67 percent ROI (accounting for all the hypervisor licenses up front in year 1):

ROI = (Gains from investment − Costs of investment) / (Costs of investment)

ROI = ($159,583.14 − $125,000.00) / $125,000.00

ROI = 27.67%

Using all the anticipated returns, the payback for this investment comes at the beginning of the third quarter of the year:

Payback = $125,000 / $159,538

Payback = 0.7832

Payback = 0.7832 * 12 months

Payback = 9.40 months

Finally, the NPV analysis also shows that spending $125,000 in hypervisor licenses is a good investment:

NPV = NPV(rate, cash flow 1, cash flow 2, cash flow 3, . . .)

NPV = NPV(0.10, 159538, 159538, 159538) − $125,000

NPV = $271,747.39

 Note

NPV analysis should be adjusted accordingly to reflect the terms of the purchase (that is, when the first cash outflow occurs) and the timelines of implementation (that is, the timing of the returns).

If only one-fourth of the infrastructure can be virtualized in one year, only one-fourth of the returns should be counted in period 1.

Disaster Recovery and Business Continuity (IaaS) Summary

Let's assume that Omicron has moved forward with its plan to virtualize its infrastructure as a part of its long-term DR strategy.

Omicron has researched cloud-hosting providers and has determined that it can purchase enough compute power to serve its business continuity and disaster recovery needs for approximately $80,000 a month. This equates to roughly 730 hours of service usage per month for 100 servers.

Therefore, Omicron can mitigate the risks and the potential costs ($500,000) associated with aforementioned five-hour outage for $960,000 annually.

Recall that their current environment is sub–four nines in terms of availability, meaning that Omicron can expect at least 53 minutes of downtime in a calendar year. Given the company's growth rate and the rapid rate of change in its environment, Omicron's management team has determined that they are at risk for at least 20 hours of unplanned downtime per year.

With those constraints in mind, the management team does the risk analysis on the additional spending required to implement a cloud-based DR strategy. Given that the downtime is not guaranteed to occur, it might make sense to do a best-worst-average case analysis.

Let's assume that 20 hours of downtime is the average-case scenario, that 10 hours of downtime is the best-case scenario, and that 30 hours of downtime is the worst-case scenario. Table 3-9 outlines the financial risk of downtime at $100,000 per outage hour.

Table 3-9   Downtime Cost Scenarios

Best-Worst-Average	Annual Downtime Costs
Cloud-based DR	($960,000.00)
Best-case estimate (10 hours)	$1,000,000.00
Average estimate (20 hours)	$2,000,000.00
Worst-case estimate (30 hours)	$3,000,000.00

In the best-case scenario, Omicron is just able to break even.

In the average-case scenario, Omicron would see an ROI of 108 percent:

ROI = (Gains from investment – Costs of investment) / (Costs of investment)

ROI = ($2,000,000 – $960,000) / $960,000

ROI = 108.33%

In the worst-case scenario, the ROI on this solution is 212.50 percent:

ROI = (Gains from investment – Costs of investment) / (Costs of investment)

ROI = ($3,000,000 – $960,000) / $960,000

ROI = 212.5%

Assuming 20 hours of downtime is virtually assured, the cloud-based DR solution appears to be a wise investment strictly based on ROI analysis.

The NPV analysis (in this case using Microsoft Excel) also vets out for the average (and worst-case) scenarios:

NPV = NPV(0.1, 2000000) – 960000

NPV = $858,181.82

Recall that the $960,000 is the annually recurring sum of the monthly charges for the cloud-based DR solution. Given that the revenue risks in the best-case scenario are almost the same as the investment—Omicron barely breaks even—the NPV on the best-case scenario is negative: –$50,909.09. If we only had the best-case scenario example as a data point, more research would be required to determine whether moving to cloud-based DR would be a good use of company funds.

Platform as a Service

Omicron management has determined that, in addition to investing in virtualized infrastructure to augment their DR strategy, they need to invest in a Platform as a Service (PaaS) offering to speed time to market (TTM) for their mobility applications.

A recent study determined that companies in Omicron's market who implemented mobile phone and tablet applications increased their revenues by an average of 5 percent over a 12-month period. By enabling researchers and customers to access Omicron's data from their handheld devices, Omicron believes it can achieve similar returns. An increase of $1.4 million in Omicron's top-line revenue could fund several infrastructure enhancements and help Omicron improve the effectiveness of its IT supply chain.

In addition to adding to Omicron's top line, an investment in mobile applications could enhance Omicron's brand recognition and potentially enable Omicron to take share from the competition.

Time to market is a critical key performance indicator for Omicron. Decreasing TTM for new applications that can augment employee productivity (like a port of their commissions and CRM applications) is a key initiative. Based on current revenues of $28 million and 100 employees, an increase of 2 percent in productivity would result in an increase in gross employee revenue productivity of $560,000 annually ($280,000 per employee * 2% * 100 employees).

Note

Here, we are using two distinct but related KPIs—total revenue and employee revenue productivity—to evaluate the benefits of investing in mobile computing platforms and applications.

As total revenues increase, assuming headcount stays flat, employee revenue productivity naturally increases as well. Therefore, it would be smart to measure the impact of mobile computing not only on total revenues and revenue per headcount, but also on the increased numbers of customer engagements, numbers of cases closed, and so on.

For the purposes of demonstration here, we look only at total revenues and revenues per headcount, with the understanding that the two metrics are obviously interrelated.

To achieve this goal of increased top-line revenue ($1.4 million or 5 percent of total revenues) and increased employee productivity of 2 percent ($560,000), Omicron plans to invest $1 million over three years in an exclusive PaaS contract with a major mobility provider. The terms of the contract are payable at the end of year 1, and the benefits and efficiencies gained in year 1 decline at a rate of 50 percent year over year.

Table 3-10 displays the total outlays and inflows from the PaaS project.

Table 3-10   Cost-Benefit Analysis of Platform as a Service Project

	Year 1	Year 2	Year 3
Total PaaS spending	($1,000,000.00)	$0.00	$0.00
Increased revenues	$1,400,000.00	$700,000.00	$350,000.00
Increased efficiencies	$560,000.00	$280,000.00	$140,000.00
Total	**$1,960,000.00**	**$980,000.00**	**$490,000.00**

Assuming that all benefits and revenues are annualized evenly (for example, there are no spikes or troughs in the timing of the returns), payback occurs just before the end of the second quarter.

The ROI in year 1 is 96 percent:

ROI = (Gains from investment – Costs of investment) / (Costs of investment)

ROI = ($1,960,000 - $1,000,000) / $1,000,000

ROI = 96%

Finally, the NPV of this investment, after accounting for 50 percent decreases in efficiencies year over year, is positive:

NPV = NPV(0.1, 1960000, 980000, 490000) − 1,000,000

NPV = $1,959,879.79

 Note

Another way of quantifying the benefits of utilizing a PaaS platform would be to estimate the timing of the revenues in terms of TTM.

For example, let's assume that using the current infrastructure, it takes Omicron 12 months to develop an application that would generate an additional $1,000,000 annually in terms of increased revenues, employee efficiencies, and cost avoidances.

If, using a PaaS platform, Omicron could build this same application in one-fourth of the time—3 months instead of 12—the inflows in terms of benefits could be accounted for quarterly. Assuming that these efficiencies are in perpetuity, three additional quarters of $250,000 inflows—an additional $750,000—could be added to the total benefits of the solution, and nine months sooner.

This is a powerful representation of why TTM is such a critical measure of performance.

Conclusion

The legacy IT supply chain has high fixed costs associated with significant capital investments in hardware and software, the use of which is often encumbered by complex, single-threaded processes. These processes, which have evolved over long periods of time, continue to hold precious compute, storage, and network resources hostage to inefficiency. These inefficiencies can severely hamper corporate performance and decrease profitability.

The adoption of cloud computing solutions mitigates or eliminates entirely many of these inefficient processes. One step toward the adoption of cloud computing is server virtualization. By virtualizing server infrastructure—and by realigning the IT supply chain to support server virtualization—significant cost reductions and avoidances can be achieved.

These cost savings or benefits—in the form of FTE realignment, utilization increases, revenue augmentation, and downtime avoidances—can be measured using before and after TCO scenarios. The business value of the benefits—the deltas between the before and the after—can be evaluated against the costs of the investments using direct metrics such as NPV, ROI, and payback analysis. In the case of measuring downtime avoidance, best-, worst-, and average-case scenarios can be used.

The Cloud Economy— The Human-Economic Impact of Cloud Computing

Given the massive economies of scale inherent in cloud computing, what is the potential impact of the adoption of cloud computing on the global economy? Extending the argument even further, what is the potential for cloud computing to impact the path of human development?

In this chapter, we cover the following topics:

- Technological Revolutions and Paradigm Change
- The Course of Human Development
- Cloud Computing as an Economic Enabler
- Cloud Computing and the Environment

Looking beyond the short-term economic recovery implications, could the widespread adoption of cloud computing improve the lives of human beings on a global scale?

In this chapter, we examine the possible effects of cloud computing on employment, economic recovery, innovation, and ultimately on human welfare. We also explore the potential of cloud computing to act as a growth enabler for both established economies and emerging markets.

Finally, we will understand how cloud computing can mitigate energy consumption and the impact of global warming through the reduction of greenhouse gases.

Technological Revolutions and Paradigm Change

If we want to estimate the longer-term and broader implications of cloud computing on the global economy and human life, it is helpful to place cloud computing in the correct historical and sociological context.

Venezuelan historian Carlota Perez, in her book *Technological Revolutions and Financial Capital, The Dynamics of Bubbles and Golden Ages*, highlights the most significant shifts in technology over the last 300 years and outlines their implications for economic and social change.

According to Perez, the blueprint for boom and bust cycles stemming from technological revolutions is inherent in capitalism. Outlining the economic impact of five major technological revolutions (the Industrial Revolution, Steam and Rail, Steel and Electric, Oil and Mass Production, and Information and Telecommunications), Perez notes the following traits common to each phase: decreased costs, increased economies of scale and scope, standardization, and the opening of a vast new territory—a *profit* or *design space*.[1]

It is significant (and pertinent to this discussion) that Perez includes the Information Revolution as one of the five major technological revolutions in the last 300 years. It is also important to note that the subsequent changes associated with these revolutions are not instantaneous. These transformations take many years to fully unfold.

Perez cites the launch of Intel's first microprocessor in 1971 as the beginning of the Information Revolution. Indeed, she opens *Technological Revolutions and Financial Capital* with this momentous event. Perez continues to note that the associated decades-long cycle of social, economic, and governmental transformation is still unfolding. The widespread adoption of cloud computing, with its enormous economies of scale and eventual standardization, can be seen as the final phase of the Information Revolution. Using Perez's timelines, we have yet another decade or two remaining before we will understand the full impact of the Information Revolution on the global economy.

---

1. Carlota Perez, *Technological Revolutions and Financial Capital, The Dynamics of Bubbles and Golden Ages*, (Cheltenham, UK: Edward Elgar, 2002), pp. 16–20. Perez notes the term *design space* is borrowed from Rikard Stankiewicz, professor emeritus, University of Lund, Sweden.

Note

In *Diffusion of Innovations*, sociologist Everett Rogers outlines the process by which new ideas, products, and processes are disseminated and adopted in a social system over time. In the case of small changes (fashion, for example), the time horizon can be very short. In the case of massive paradigm shifts—such as the shift from costly, private computing resources to scalable, affordable public resources (that is, the cloud)—the time horizon is far longer.

The process of cloud computing adoption in corporate IT departments follows Rogers' process of *agenda-setting*, *matching*, *redefining/restructuring*, *clarifying*, and *routinizing*.[2] For large organizations with highly populated chains of command, this process can take several years.

As the business and operational processes in the IT supply chain adapt to cloud computing service models, the rate of adoption of cloud computing will accelerate.

The Course of Human Development

With this sociological and historical context in mind, and with an understanding of the timelines and phases of technology adoption, it is possible to estimate the economic impact of cloud computing in terms of improved quality of life and human development.

Much of economics is based on the concept of scarce or limited resources. We live in a world where a minority of the population has tremendous advantages relative to the majority. Established economies share similar structural fundamentals that provide a continuum of advantages and propel the overall economy forward. The majority of citizens living in First World economies typically have easy access to clean water, for example, while many human beings (nearly one-seventh of the world's population) lack safe drinking water. Safe and robust infrastructure coupled with strong governance and legal systems are all critical for the ongoing success of an economy and, by extension, a society.

Just as there is an economic impact to expanding production processes (generally speaking, at least marginally increased output is expected), applying technology to business problems can also yield a net positive economic impact. Increased production comes with increased costs unless there are economies of scale at work. The economies of scale associated with cloud computing can reduce both fixed and

---

2.   Everett Rogers, *Diffusion of Innovations*, 4th Edition, p. 392.

variable costs of production. In short, migrating to the cloud can restructure the economic inputs in the IT supply chain to allow both greater outputs and reduced costs.

Just as the use of cloud computing can reduce capital expenditures (CAPEX) and operating expenditures (OPEX) in the IT supply chain, on a much larger scale, the adoption of cloud computing by public and private organizations can lead to the simplification of the many complex value chains required to support human life and development. The economies of scale associated with cloud computing can reduce firms' power consumption and their consequent carbon footprint. The reduction of costs in the supply chain can simplify and speed the process of innovation, which in turn can create additional employment opportunities, decrease time to market for lifesaving drugs, and help provide access to clean water and shelter.

The United Nations Human Development Index

For each of the last 21 years, the United Nations Human Development Report Office (HDRO) has issued the Human Development Index (HDI), measuring the correlation between economic growth in the world's nations and overall human development.

The 2011 report, titled "Sustainability and Equity: A Better Future for All," ties sustainability to economic growth, recognizing that in many countries, economic gain (pure income growth) has come at the cost of the environment.

Building sustainable global business models to fund the provision of clean water and sanitation, low carbon and renewable energy, and other processes to address climate change is a tall order by any calculation. The UN HDRO estimates this will be a multitrillion dollar annual expenditure through 2030.[3] Ensuring that governmental policies and regulations support sustainability programs can be even more challenging than funding these efforts given obvious conflicts of interests. Consider the following contradiction: The 2011 report outlines how in many countries fossil fuel subsidies far outpace health subsidies. Yet, the health benefits associated with clean air, water, and energy would more than offset the required expenditures to fund renewable energy sources over time.

Many groups advocate creative methods—a mixture of microcredit, commercial finance, public subsidies, grants, and taxes (the 2011 report highlights a proposal for a currency transaction tax)—to close the funding gap for the technologies and R&D required to improve quality of life and support sustainability efforts. Is it possible then, in this light, to use the advantages associated with cloud computing as a type of economic engine to assist with the trillions of dollars required to achieve the goals outlined by the United Nations?

---

3. Source: United Nations Human Development Index, United Nations Human Development Report Office, UNDI 2011, Chapter 5, page 91.

Using the UNHDI as a backdrop, let us turn to the potential broader benefits of cloud computing as applied to the economies of the world.

Cloud Computing as an Economic Enabler

It is easy to be pessimistic about the current state of the global economy. Unemployment has reached critical status in many of the established economies. Across the European Union, job creation has faltered as the Eurozone debt crisis worsens. As of November 2011, seasonally adjusted unemployment in Spain was more than 22 percent, while in Ireland and Portugal, the percent of the population unemployed was more than 14 percent and 12 percent, respectively.[4]

With unemployment in the United States at 8.5 percent at the end of December 2011—the total number of unemployed in the United States totaled just over 13 million—job creation remains a critical issue in advance of the 2012 presidential election.[5]

Commenting on U.S. employment statistics in their work *Race Against the Machine*, Erik Brynjolfsson (Schussel Family Professor at the MIT Sloan School of Management and director of the MIT Center for Digital Business) and Andrew McAfee (principal research scientist at MIT's Center for Digital Business) observed, "the mean length of time unemployed had skyrocketed to 39.9 weeks by the middle of 2011, a duration almost twice as long as that observed during any previous postwar recovery. And the workforce participation rate, or proportion of working-age adults with jobs, fell below 64 percent—a level not seen since 1983 when women had not yet entered the labor force in large numbers."[6]

In the years between 2008 and 2010, the U.S. Gross Domestic Product (GDP) averaged a growth rate of 1.2 percent versus an average of 5.2 percent between 2000 and 2007.[7]

---

4. Bureau of Labor Statistics, "International Unemployment Rates and Employment Indexes, Seasonally Adjusted, 2007–2011," www.bls.gov/fls/intl_unemployment_rates_monthly.htm, accessed January 2012.

5. Bureau of Labor Statistics, "Employment Situation Summary," www.bls.gov/news.release/empsit.nr0.htm, accessed January 2012.

6. Brynjolfsson, Erik; McAfee, Andrew (2011-10-17). *Race Against The Machine: How the Digital Revolution is Accelerating Innovation, Driving Productivity, and Irreversibly Transforming Employment and the Economy* (Kindle Locations 48–54). Digital Frontier Press. Kindle Edition.

7. Bureau of Economic Analysis, "National Economic Accounts, GDP," www.bea.gov/national/index.htm#gdp, accessed January 2012.

Taking a broader view, the first decade of the new millennium showed an average growth of 3.9 percent, the lowest 10-year average since before World War II. (Note: The years leading up to Y2K were the second-worst performing in terms of GDP).[8] Average United States GDP by decade (in current and chained 2005 dollars) is shown in Table 4-1.

Table 4-1   Average United States GDP by Decade

Years	Current Dollars	Chained 2005 Dollars
1930–1940	0.7	2.0
1941–1950	11.7	6.0
1951–1960	6.1	3.6
1961–1970	7.1	4.2
1971–1980	10.4	3.2
1981–1990	7.6	3.3
1991–2000	5.6	3.4
2001–2010	3.9	1.6

The economic crisis in the United States, including the housing crisis (associated with the subprime lending scandal) and the financial meltdown of 2008, can certainly be blamed for a reasonable share of capital and productivity erosion: The years 2008 and 2009 averaged a net negative 0.5 percent retraction in GDP. The percent change in U.S. GDP between 2000 and 2010 is shown in Table 4-2.

Table 4-2   United States GDP Percent Change from 2000 to 2010

Years	Current Dollars	Chained 2005 Dollars
2000	6.4	4.1
2001	3.4	1.1
2002	3.5	1.8
2003	4.7	2.5
2004	6.4	3.5

8.   Ibid.

Years	Current Dollars	Chained 2005 Dollars
2005	6.5	3.1
2006	6.0	2.7
2007	4.9	1.9
2008	1.9	−0.3
2009	−2.5	−3.5
2010	4.2	3.0

While 2010 showed forward movement in terms of U.S. GDP, it is fair to say that the United States is still in the middle of a protracted economic course correction: U.S. GDP was revised downward to 1.8 percent in the third quarter of 2011.[9] As the Eurozone attempts to unwind its own debt situation, the E.U. might well be heading for its own double-dip recession.[10] Clear signs of global economic recovery remain elusive at this point in time.

 Note

For consistency's sake, I reference GDP here, but note that many economists, as well as thought leaders from other disciplines, believe that the use of GDP as a measure of economic health and progress is fundamentally flawed. The use of Gross National Income (GNI) is often recommended as a better indicator of a nation's ability to provide a high quality of life for its citizens.

The data then leads us to a fundamental question: Can cloud computing offer any assistance to the problem of job creation? Or is the use of advanced computing technologies putting more jobs at risk?

Cloud Computing and Unemployment

Let's be honest: There is a perception that cloud computing will reduce, if not eliminate, a number of IT and IT-related jobs. Certainly, when we talk of lowering

9.   Trading Economics, "United States GDP Growth Rate," www.tradingeconomics.com/united-states/gdp-growth, accessed January 2012.

10.   Yahoo! Finance, Associated Press, "EU Warns of Possible Recession in Eurozone," http://finance.yahoo.com/news/eu-warns-possible-recession-eurozone-093842534.html, accessed January 2012.

full-time equivalent (FTE) charges in conjunction with "automating the IT supply chain," the perception that cloud computing might put some people out of work is not unwarranted. Assuming that cloud computing will not eliminate certain IT positions (at least in the near term), it is reasonable to assume that cloud computing will permanently alter some computing job roles and responsibilities as we have come to know them.

 Note

Anecdotally speaking, how many computing jobs were eliminated during the transition from the mainframe era to open systems computing? How many skilled mainframe operators were unable to make the jump from the mainframe to client-server platforms? A few perhaps. Alternatively, how many more simply retired when the option to do so became available? The data does not provide a clear answer to this question.

Given the broad organizational impact of cloud computing—the dismantling of the silos in the IT supply chain—what might the restructuring of computing employment subsequent to cloud adoption look like?

The most recent survey conducted by the Bureau of Labor Statistics on employment and mean wages by the largest occupations highlights the roles and responsibilities of what it refers to as the "information super-sector."

In terms of both numbers of employees and mean wages, software developers (both for systems and applications) and computer support specialists are in the top ten of the information super-sector. Telecom equipment installers and repairers and telecom line installers and repairers are in the top three. Table 4-3 shows the employment and mean wage data for the top ten occupations in the information super-sector.

Table 4-3   Employment and Mean Wages for the Information Super-Sector, May 2010[11]

Occupation	Employment	Average Annual Wage	Percent of Sector Employment
Customer service representatives	164,180	$36,180	6.10
Telecommunications equipment installers and repairers, except line installers	141,130	$54,440	5.20

11. Bureau of Labor Statistics, "Occupational Employment Statistics," www.bls.gov/oes/current/occ_industry.htm, accessed January 2012.

Occupation	Employment	Average Annual Wage	Percent of Sector Employment
Telecommunications line installers and repairers	104,430	$53,530	3.90
Sales representatives, services, all others	95,200	$60,570	3.50
Advertising sales agents	81,510	$50,850	3.00
Software developers, applications	74,950	$93,170	2.80
Editors	70,950	$59,620	2.60
Computer support specialists	67,390	$51,730	2.50
Software developers, systems software	55,880	$97,340	2.10
Producers and directors	55,670	$93,300	2.10

The combined annual average wage for these five categories (system and application developers, computer support specialists, and telecom equipment and line repairers and installers) is nearly $30 billion. If the adoption of cloud computing were to eliminate a significant number of these positions, the impact to the U.S. economy would be catastrophic.

I would argue, however, that in the near term, the market shift to cloud computing will preserve many if not most of these positions, because of the complex nature of the legacy systems in place, and because of the length of time required to migrate to new platforms without impactful disruptions of service.

In the long term, the picture is less clear. Using our legacy IT supply chain model as a frame of reference, what might a similar employment survey look like 20 years from now when the migration to cloud computing is complete?

Supply chain efficiencies and economies of scale achieved by implementing both private cloud and public cloud infrastructures could potentially reduce the numbers of individuals assigned to hardware configuration, for example. These same efficiencies, however, might very well increase the numbers of individuals required for application support. (After the supply chain is flattened, the time to market [TTM] for applications will be vastly reduced; therefore the capacity to build more applications will increase.)

Automated provisioning in the long term might well reduce requirements for certain positions. Indeed, as the legacy silos collapse and as "push-button" functionality becomes a reality for provisioning, the need for individuals dedicated to entitlement verification and resource assignment will be diminished.

Other positions listed in the information super-sector—line installers and repairers, for example—could be subject to marginal reductions as mergers and acquisitions continue, but the overall need for line repairers and installers does not go away. Likewise, as businesses focus on applications and consumer usage continues to grow, the need for software developers will grow accordingly. In fact, as the speed of application development and deployment increases, the need for talented software developers should increase as well. Using our IT supply chain example once more, you can almost picture the backlog of applications being released to the market as the bullwhip effect is rectified and access to free or nearly free computing resources is made widely available on demand.

Twenty years from now (if not sooner), we can imagine that the Bureau of Labor Statistics will have a completely separate categorization for *cloud computing* (or *computing utility* or *computing distribution*) specialties as the industry continues to shift and mature.

As time horizons increase beyond the next few decades, however, the visibility into job creation and preservation related to the adoption of cloud computing diminishes greatly. Keeping in mind Moore's Law, can we say with any assurance that continued advances in technology won't eliminate a percentage of certain roles? As Erik Brynjolfsson and Andrew McAfee outline in *Race Against the Machine*, to keep pace with Moore's dictum individuals and institutions must continually work to maintain their relevance and value to society. Think of walking up a down escalator: Unless you take two steps or more at a time, you will ride it all the way to the bottom.

 Note

The discussion around cloud computing and the job market is invariably intertwined with the discussion of "offshoring" or "outsourcing" of call-center and other IT-related positions. When we picture a market, be it a job market or a market for a new product, all things being equal (*ceteris paribus*), profit seekers will follow cost reductions.

For example, assume that there is a market opportunity for some type of good or service. Two distinct, viable business models target this market—one with 10 percent profit margins, and one with 20 percent profit margins. Unilaterally, bidders will favor the business model with 20 percent profit margins.

In a global economy where falling labor prices and offshoring initiatives enable higher margins (even incrementally higher margins), localized job loss or job migration is a risk.

Free markets seek equilibrium. As inflation becomes a risk in China and other offshoring capitals, we might see U.S. profit centers reclaiming lost jobs if profits can be maintained or increased.[12]

Fears of massive job cuts related to the adoption of cloud computing, however, run counter to current research.

Mike Schüssler and Jasson Urbach, in their paper titled "The Economic Impact of Cloud Computing in South Africa," highlight how cloud computing reduces the costs required to create a job. Current numbers indicate that the "South African economy requires R2.2 million for every eight jobs. While using the same capital in real terms this study finds that the amount of jobs that R2.2 million can provide would increase to 8.1. While this is not a significant increase it indicates that for every 80,000 jobs that the South African economy creates on its previous capital to labour ratio—at a cost of R22 billion, cloud computing could potentially add about an extra 1,000 jobs. One must remember that these extra jobs would not cost the economy an extra cent."[13]

The economies of scale associated with cloud computing reduce the total capital costs—think back to Porter's value chain and our IT supply chain analogy—required for the same amount of output. Therefore, as cloud computing platforms are adopted, cloud computing can, in fact, act as a job engine.

Federico Etro, professor of economics at the University of Venice, Ca' Foscari, has published widely on many macroeconomic topics including competition, market structures, and research and development. In "The Economic Consequences of the

---

12. The Telegraph, "World power swings back to America," www.telegraph.co.uk/finance/comment/ambroseevans_pritchard/8844646/World-power-swings-back-to-America.html, accessed January 2012.

13. Mike Schüssler and Jasson Urbach, "The Economic Impact of Cloud Computing in South Africa," The Freemarket Foundation, Johannesburg, www.freemarketfoundation.com/DynamicData/Event_45.pdf.

Diffusion of Cloud Computing," Etro highlights how cloud computing will reduce "the fixed costs of entry and production by shifting capital expenditure in ICT [Information and Communications Technology] into operative costs."[14] In other words, as the costs of computing and telecom infrastructure required to build and run a business are reduced, the costs of creating new jobs are also reduced.

To summarize at a much higher level, a percentage of the roles classically associated with departmental computing might shift as cloud adoption increases, but given the current visibility, it would be egregiously speculative to argue that cloud computing will eliminate a significant number of computing jobs over the next decade.[15]

Cloud Computing and the Environment

The data center industry has long been a target of technology innovation because of the size and scale of problems that data center owners and managers typically face. Data center facilities often cover tens to hundreds of thousands of square feet while consuming multiple megawatts of power. Inefficiencies in a supply chain this large can waste multiple millions of dollars annually. A 10 percent CPU utilization rate in a huge data center facility easily translates into not only process inefficiency—OPEX charges relating to the management of thousands of servers—but also into OPEX and CAPEX spending associated with energy consumption and poor hardware utilization rates. Correspondingly, as you can probably imagine, the cost efficiencies to be gained from implementing cloud computing at this scale are immense. Likewise, the potential reduction in carbon footprints is also significant.

In early 2011, Microsoft, in conjunction with Accenture and WSP Environment and Energy, commissioned a study on energy consumption and cloud computing. The study concluded that large companies could see reductions in their carbon footprint of 30 percent or more and that smaller companies could see reductions on the order of 90 percent.[16]

In July 2011, the Carbon Disclosure Project released a study (conducted by the independent research firm Verdantix and sponsored by AT&T) titled "Cloud Computing:

---

14. Federico Etro, "The Economic Consequences of the Diffusion of Cloud Computing," 2010 World Economic Forum, The Global Information Technology Report 2009–2010.

15. Mergers and acquisitions across the telecommunications sector and computing and networking industry are a different story, of course. Synergies often cited as reasons for acquisitions typically include the elimination of redundant roles.

16. Sustainable Industries, "Sustainability in the Cloud," http://sustainableindustries.com/articles/2011/01/sustainability-cloud, accessed January 2012.

The IT Solution for the 21st Century."[17] Verdantix used data from 11 companies across multiple sectors in the United States to determine the potential financial impact of cloud computing. The study concluded that by the year 2020, widespread adoption of cloud computing by the largest companies in the United States could result in an annual energy savings of $12.3 billion.[18] Projections show that U.S. firms with revenues greater than $1 billion plan to spend 69 percent of their budget on infrastructure, platform, and software budgets on cloud services by 2020 and could cut 85.7 million metric tons of CO2 per year in the process.[19]

In an email interview with Stuart Neumann, the senior manager at Verdantix in charge of the study, Stuart stated that a similar study was completed for France and the U.K., and annual energy savings of $1.2 billion and $2 billion, respectively, were forecast.[20]

While the savings associated with a wider adoption of cloud computing cannot be ignored, Neumann believes that security concerns are still an adoption inhibitor for many customers in the short term. Increased innovation and greater assumption of liability are required by cloud providers before more customers, especially those with serious security concerns, will move to the cloud.[21]

When asked whether cloud computing could help enable a more meritocratic approach to the sciences, Neumann asserted that cloud computing puts more computing power into the hands of smaller companies with perhaps less funding. The potential for increased compute power at a lower cost could lead to increased potential for innovation.[22]

Meritocratic Applications of Cloud Computing

A well-known example of the meritocratic application of computing power is the World Community Grid. As part of the World Community Grid, end users enroll their devices (laptops, workstations, and so on) in the grid program. After enrollment, a small software program is installed on the device, permitting that device

---

17. Carbon Disclosure Project, "Cloud Computing: The IT Solution for the 21st Century," http://content.yudu.com/A1t6nj/Cloud-Computing, accessed January 2012.

18. Environmental Leader, "CDP Cloud Computing Can Save $12bn," www.environmentalleader.com/2011/07/20/cdp-cloud-computing-can-save-12bn, accessed January 2012.

19. Verdantix, "Verdantix Cloud Computing Report For Carbon Disclosure Project Forecasts $12.3 Billion Financial Savings For US Firms," www.verdantix.com/index.cfm/papers/Press.Details/press_id/58/verdantix-cloud-computing-report-for-carbon-disclosure-project-forecasts-12-3-billion-financial-savings-for-us-firms/-, accessed January 2012.

20. Email interview conducted in September 2011.

21. Ibid.

22. Ibid.

to become part of a massively scalable distributed grid of compute resources. The World Community Grid can then utilize that device's spare computational cycles to process huge amounts of data required to solve scientific problems critical to human-kind.

The Grid's first project, Human Proteome Folding, was begun in 2003. Since then, other projects have included Nutritious Rice for the World, Discovering Dengue Drugs Together, and African Climate Home. The World Community Grid sponsors many ongoing efforts to help cure cancer, muscular dystrophy, AIDS, and other life-threatening illnesses.[23]

While technically not cloud computing—recall our previous definitions of cloud service models—the World Community Grid does give us an example of what is capable with easy access to enormous amounts of inexpensive computing power.

Speaking strictly of the cloud, pharmaceutical company Eli Lilly has used Amazon Web Services and other cloud computing platforms to decrease total time to market. In an interview with *Information Week* in January 2009, Lilly veteran Dave Powers discussed how server-provisioning time was trimmed from months to minutes.[24]

Drug maker Pfizer has also documented its adoption of virtual private cloud (VPC) or hybrid cloud technologies with Amazon Web Services. In an interview with *BioPharma News* in June 2010, Michael Miller, senior director of High Performance Computing and R&D, outlined how Pfizer can condense weeks of computations down to hours.[25]

When the difference between first and last to market can mean multiple millions of dollars in revenues, time to market is a critical measurement of success or failure. If cloud computing can enable increased profits and revenues while reducing costs, is it really a significant leap to state that cloud computing can increase overall quality of life for individuals in less established economies?

As the data and our examples have shown, public and privately held companies alike can reduce overall expenses (both CAPEX and OPEX), reduce time to market (TTM), and generate significant returns on investments by adopting cloud computing technologies. How then should we measure the broader impact of cloud adoption on human welfare?

---

23. The World Community Grid, www.worldcommunitygrid.org, accessed January 2012.

24. *Information Week*, "Eli Lilly on what's next in the cloud," www.informationweek.com/cloud-computing/blog/archives/2009/01/whats_next_in_t.html, accessed January 2012.

25. *BioPharma News*, http://biopharmadirectory.com/news/?p=159, accessed November 2011.

Alternative Metrics and Measures of Welfare

Measuring the anticipated benefits of cloud computing implementations with traditional business metrics is a fundamental step of furthering the adoption of cloud computing. (To be sure, most investments in cloud computing will not happen without some sort of business case or financial justification.) Successful cloud implementations—those that show the creation of true business value—will also in turn accelerate the adoption of cloud computing. The standardization of cloud interfaces and the certification of major applications will be an indicator of the diffusion rate of the cloud paradigm. As outlined previously, the widespread adoption of cloud computing will take time. However, with the certification of major software platforms such as Oracle and SAP on Amazon Web Services, those timelines are quickly becoming compressed.[26]

If we look at the cycles and timelines outlined by Perez, we can estimate that cloud computing adoption (as a final phase of the microchip and ICT revolution) has at a minimum another decade in which to impact corporate computing. The impact of cloud adoption will extend to social, legal, and governmental frameworks as well. In fact, the potential effects of cloud adoption are so large and so far-reaching, it could be argued that cloud computing is its own technological revolution. Regardless, cloud computing is *at least* the base enabler of a new phase of technological advancement, one in which corporations, governments, and societies alike are becoming dependent upon free (or nearly free) and ubiquitous computing resources. As part of this phase of history, it will be incumbent upon leaders and decision makers to determine how best to use these powerful resources to the greatest benefit.

As we have seen, traditional measurements of technology implementations (ROI, BPE, NPV, and so on) can be used successfully to justify investments in cloud platforms. Given the broader implications of cloud adoption, however, perhaps it is necessary to project the impact of cloud computing on society using certain alternative metrics as well.

There are numerous alternative measurements of economic performance in use today. Academics and policy makers have increasingly advocated for an alternative to GDP (the sum total of all goods and services exchanged) to measure the health and productivity of an economy. In addition to omitting items like household labor, the depletive effects of sacrificing natural resources to boost short-term growth are not taken into account with traditional GDP calculations. Clear-cutting forests, for example, can result in higher numbers for new home starts and increased production and revenues for paper products in years 1 and 2, but can result in widespread erosion and reduced production in years 10 and 11. Under the current GDP rubric,

---

26. Amazon Web Services, "Global Solution Providers," http://aws.amazon.com/solutions/global-solution-providers, accessed January 2012.

there is no facility for measuring and correlating future negative costs associated with increased revenues and profits in the present, and therefore no ability to measure the sustainability of economic growth.

Ecological economists (such as the Chilean Manfred Max-Neef) have long argued for a more comprehensive understanding of the relationship of human needs to economic growth. The notion of a "threshold hypothesis" comes from the belief that as free markets grow beyond a certain size, the costs from that growth ultimately outweigh the benefits. Alternative metrics like the Index of Sustainable Economic Welfare (IESW), Genuine Progress Indicator (GPI), and Sustainable Net Benefit Index (SNBI) seek to quantitatively capture the value of growth in an economy relative to the negative costs of that growth.[27]

Can we tie the impact of cloud computing to the advancement of human welfare? Perhaps the most useful first step would be the addition of a "contribution component" to measure the contribution of cloud computing to a commonly accepted standard of measurement. We have already examined the United Nations' Human Development Index (HDI), which measures life expectancy at birth, education, and gross national income per capita.[28] It would be a fairly academic exercise to add a variable to capture the contribution of cloud computing to each of the indicators (knowledge, health, labor, and so on) that are built in to the HDI.

Obviously, we are talking about a multiyear process—moving from simple commercial acceptance of new computing models to measuring improvements in life expectancy, poverty, and empowerment by the consumption of cloud cycles. However, it is conceivable that cloud computing could become the enabler for what economist David C. Korten calls a "just and sustainable New Economy."[29]

Certainly, it would be more than problematic to shift business performance metrics in the private sector to reflect and reward altruistic uses of technology. Imagine altering our current Generally Accepted Accounting Principles and revenue-reporting processes to quantify technological contributions to GPI. How long would that process take, assuming that it could be done at all?

The onus then falls to the public sector and the governing bodies of the world to ensure that policies supporting sustainable growth are encouraged equitably and across the board.

---

27. Philip A. Lawn, "A theoretical foundation to support the Index of Sustainable Economic Welfare (ISEW), Genuine Progress Indicator (GPI), and other related indexes," Ecological Economics 44 (2003) 105/118, Elsevier, 2003.

28. UNDP, Human Development Reports, "Human Development Index (HDI)," http://hdr.undp.org/en/statistics/hdi, accessed January 2012.

29. David C. Korten, "Path to a Just and Sustainable New Economy," Revised and expanded version of a presentation delivered to The EU Club of Rome, Brussels, January 26, 2010.

The minimum funding required to begin addressing climate change, provide clean water and sanitation, and supply renewable, low-carbon energy (as outlined by the UN HDI) approaches $40 billion annually. Given the enormity of the need, could the widespread adoption of cloud computing in each world economy, subsidized by local and federal government investments, generate returns sufficient to close this gap? The data leads us to believe so.

The funding options are potentially limitless. Portions of cloud offsets could be placed in an "innovation" or "climate fund." Carbon offsets related to cloud computing usage could be traded on the open market with proceeds earmarked for reinvestment in cloud infrastructure or services. Economic credits could be utilized as incentives to adopt cloud computing. Or, to take a more punitive stance, "legacy taxes" could be levied against companies not using cloud computing.

If, by adopting cloud computing, the largest companies in the United States could generate returns of $12 billion and carbon offsets equal to 200 million barrels of oil *annually* (as the Verdantix study shows), what type of funding could be amassed if world authorities were to subsidize a cloud agenda on the global economic stage? It is not hard to imagine a scenario where increased productivity levels (and profits) in established economies could raise productivity levels—and the overall quality of life—in emerging economies.

Could we—by authoring a global *currency of compute*—create a universal political identity and usher in an unprecedented era of sustainability that supports growth in emerging economies but does not hinder growth in established economies?[30] I believe the answer is yes.

The Economic Future of Cloud Computing

We have seen that cloud computing is part of a broader technological revolution that began in the early 1970s. In this historical context, we have highlighted how business metrics can be used to justify and measure the returns of cloud computing implementations.

A strong understanding of customers' current environments (the before picture), including software licensing, growth rates, energy consumption, storage, and network usage, is required as a baseline.

Stuart Neumann from Verdantix adds that, "If a firm is considering moving from a traditional ERP solution to a cloud-based application, they would need to ensure they understand the following aspects of their operation to build an appropriate

---

30. Historian Benedict Anderson outlined in *Imagined Communities* how the evolution of the novel and the newspaper led to the construction of national consciousness by the creation of an identity relative to time. Could it be possible to construct an identity relative to cloud computing power and its concomitant benefits?

business case: hardware costs, software license fee costs, electricity costs, maintenance and support. The number of employees (and therefore associated costs) who are actually involved in providing maintenance and support is often one of the most challenging aspects for firms as they can be supporting multiple applications."[31]

While understanding the before picture is essential, understanding the "during picture" is equally critical.

Neumann continues, "As well as this, the firm would also need to calculate the cost of transitioning to a cloud model (data migration, training, headcount reduction). This would need to be balanced with the costs required to roll out a new version of the existing ERP application, which is generally required by firms every five years. These costs include hardware purchase, data migration, system customization, training, license fees and implementation costs. These would be avoided costs if a firm moved to a cloud-based service but would still need to go into the business case."[32]

As demonstrated previously, these cost avoidances in terms of both CAPEX and OPEX can quickly add up to millions of dollars annually.

We have discussed how economies of scale associated with cloud computing can positively impact both the private and public sectors. We have also examined the potential broader economic impact of cloud computing with respect to job creation. While the longer-term—20-plus years or more—impact of cloud computing on employment is less clear, the cost reductions associated with cloud computing can, in the short term, reduce the cost of creating new jobs, enabling cloud computing to act as a job engine.

It is important to understand the differences between cloud computing and outsourcing. While there are certainly areas of overlap—an outsourcing model can include individual or multiple components of a cloud computing strategy—they do not always equal each other.

As Verdantix's Neumann points out, "Cloud computing can certainly be a form of outsourcing. For example, if you choose to use a third party to provide an infrastructure or platform cloud service, you are essentially outsourcing the provision and management of these elements of your IT to another organization. However, outsourcing and offshoring are certainly not the same as cloud computing. Cloud computing is a multifaceted concept and needs to be understood in terms of its characteristics (for example, server virtualization, self-service, capabilities available over a network), service delivery model (for example, IaaS, PaaS, SaaS) and deployment model (for example, public, private, hybrid). While an outsource of a company's IT

---

31. Email interview, September 2011.

32. Ibid.

can result in it being delivered as a cloud service, it could equally be delivered in the same way as before but by employees from another company."[33]

The adoption of cloud computing has the potential to impact a number of related and nonrelated technologies. We have already seen how the early-stage adoption of cloud computing platforms such as Amazon Web Services has enabled significant reductions in computing cycles required to perform the same workloads versus legacy environments. The ability for cloud computing to streamline the research and development of new medicines cannot be overstated.

The reduction in overall CAPEX and OPEX associated with cloud computing diminishes the barriers to entry for new firms, enabling startups to have equal footing with established players in terms of computing power. Removing the cost barriers for computing, and essentially flattening the IT supply chain, levels the playing field for innovation.

I'd like to close with one final complementary viewpoint on innovation. We have spent a great deal of time examining how customers' adoptions of cloud computing will affect their operational and financial performance. In a recent interchange with Dante Malagrinó, CEO and cofounder of Embrane, the potential impact of cloud computing on technology providers came up. "A fundamental difference that cloud computing introduces," Dante relayed, "is a change in the requirements for the devices that enable and support the cloud. ... Traditional products and architectures were not designed according to [cloud] requirements, and it's practically impossible to retrofit them for the cloud. Thus, vendors who want to participate in building cloud computing data centers will have to compete on an equal footing. This clearly favors innovation and levels the playing field."

Innovation and adoption are two recurring themes that echo throughout this discussion. The simple fact of the matter is that innovation and adoption are two sides of the same coin. As we move through the journey to cloud over the coming years, it is critical that we remind ourselves that just as there is only one coin, there is only one human population with the potential to benefit greatly from this historic technological revolution.

---

33. Ibid.

Conclusion

C.K. Prahalad's 2005 classic *The Fortune at the Bottom of the Pyramid* clearly documents the market opportunity for goods and services that address the needs of the world's poor (those living on less than $2 per day). Prahalad's research debunks the idea that the poor have no purchasing power, underscoring the exact opposite: Experimentation and innovation in these markets can lead to significant returns.

Addressing the needs of the poor is a tremendous opportunity, not only in terms of potential profits for successful companies and entrepreneurs but also in terms of reestablishing dignity for an often-overlooked population.

As the decreased costs of computing and increased availability of bandwidth (coupled with the ubiquity of the mobile handset) foster the growth of mobile money, mobile health, and mobile agriculture in emerging economies, the need for global oversight and governance becomes increasingly critical. The democratization of computing and network technologies means that efforts to improve human welfare will no longer be blocked by issues like physical access or entitlement. The issues that will continue to plague human progress are timeworn and two-fold: greed and corruption. Mobile and cloud technologies are not capable of addressing the corrupt practices and underlying greed contributing to inadequate supplies of food and shelter in both emerging and established economies.

The widespread adoption of cloud computing (and the associated economies of scale, which reduce the barriers to innovation) has the potential to fundamentally change the global economic landscape as we know it today. Profitable, sustainable business models focused on the needs of the world's poor can create long-term growth and enable global economic recovery. The coupling of the two—innovative business models and cloud computing—along with strong governance, presents a good base from which decision makers can work to confront worldwide gaps in clean, low-carbon energy; sanitation; and safe drinking water. Addressing these needs on a global basis could be greatest return of all from implementing cloud computing.

References

Works Cited

Chapter 1

Simon Crosby, Xensource and David Brown, Sun Microsystems. "The Virtualization Reality: Are hypervisors the new foundation for system software?" Available at http://queue.acm.org/detail.cfm?id=1189289, accessed January 2012.

Brynjolfsson, Erik; McAfee, Andrew (2011-10-17). *Race Against The Machine: How the Digital Revolution is Accelerating Innovation, Driving Productivity, and Irreversibly Transforming Employment and the Economy* (Kindle Locations 286–289). Digital Frontier Press. Kindle Edition.

National Institute of Standards and Technology, "NIST Definition of Cloud Computing." www.nist.gov/itl/cloud/upload/cloud-def-v15.pdf. Accessed December 2011.

Michael E. Porter, *Competitive Advantage: Creating and Sustaining Superior Performance*, The Free Press, New York, 1985, pp. 41–44.

Hau L. Lee, V. Padmanabhan, and Seungjin Whang. "The Bullwhip Effect in Supply Chains." MIT Sloan Management Review. http://sloanreview.mit.edu/the-magazine/1997-spring/3837/the-bullwhip-effect-in-supply-chains. Accessed December 2011.

Cachon, Randall, and Schmidt. "In Search of the Bullwhip Effect." Manufacturing & Service Operations Management 9(4), pp. 457–479. INFORMS. http://opim.wharton.upenn.edu/~cachon/pdf/bwv2.pdf. Accessed January 2012.

Huang, Z. and Palvia, P. "ERP Implementation Issues in Advanced and Developing Countries." *Business Process Management Journal.* Vol 7, No 3, 2001, pp. 276–284. See also "Why ERP may not be Suitable for Organisations in Developing Countries in Asia," by Rajapakse, Jayanatha, and Seddon, Peter B.

The Colocation Service Provider Directory, www.colocationprovider.org/ whatiscolocation.htm. Accessed December 2011.

7Economy Global Economy Library, "Cloud Computing: PaaS: Application Development and Deployment Platform in the Cloud," http://7economy.com/ archives/6857. Accessed December 2011.

Terremark's most recent 10-K filing: www.faqs.org/sec-filings/100614/ TERREMARK-WORLDWIDE-INC_10-K.

Chapter 2

Google, Inc. Google Apps Service Level Agreement, www.google.com/apps/intl/en/ terms/sla.html. Accessed December 2011.

Amazon's EC2 Service Level Agreement, http://aws.amazon.com/ec2-sla. Accessed January 2012.

Ho, Lin C. "How to Apply 6 Sigma Quality Practices to Your Business," E-Week. com, www.eweek.com/c/a/IT-Management/How-to-Apply-Six-Sigma-Quality-Practices-to-Your-Business. Accessed December 2011.

Stephen A. Ross, Randolph W. Westerfield, and Jeffrey Jaffe, *Corporate Finance,* Fifth Edition. New York: Irwin/McGraw-Hill, 1999, p. 65.

Microsoft Office Help, "NPV," http://office.microsoft.com/en-us/sharepoint-foundation-help/npv-function-HA010380009.aspx?CTT=1. Accessed January 2012.

Chapter 3

George Reese. *Cloud Application Architectures.* Sebastapol, CA: O'Reilly Media, Inc. 2009, pp. 52–53.

Microsoft Office Help, "IRR," http://office.microsoft.com/en-us/excel-help/ irr-HP005209146.aspx. Accessed December 2011.

Chapter 4

Carlota Perez, *Technological Revolutions and Financial Capital, The Dynamics of Bubbles and Golden Ages.* Cheltenham, UK: Edward Elgar, 2002, pp. 16–20.

Everett Rogers, *Diffusion of Innovations*, 4th Edition. New York: The Free Press, A Division of Simon and Schuster Inc., 1995, p. 392.

Source: United Nations Human Development Index, United Nations Human Development Report Office, UNDI 2011, Chapter 5, page 91.

Bureau of Labor Statistics, "International Unemployment Rates and Employment Indexes, Seasonally Adjusted, 2007–2011." www.bls.gov/fls/intl_unemployment_rates_monthly.htm. Accessed January 2012.

Bureau of Labor Statistics, "Employment Situation Summary." www.bls.gov/news.release/empsit.nr0.htm. Accessed January 2012.

Brynjolfsson, Erik; McAfee, Andrew (2011-10-17). *Race Against The Machine: How the Digital Revolution is Accelerating Innovation, Driving Productivity, and Irreversibly Transforming Employment and the Economy*. Digital Frontier Press. Kindle Edition.

Bureau of Economic Analysis, "National Economic Accounts, GDP," www.bea.gov/national/index.htm#gdp. Accessed January 2012.

Trading Economics, "United States GDP Growth Rate," www.tradingeconomics.com/united-states/gdp-growth. Accessed January 2012.

Yahoo! Finance, Associated Press, "EU Warns of Possible Recession in Eurozone," http://finance.yahoo.com/news/eu-warns-possible-recession-eurozone-093842534.html. Accessed January 2012.

Bureau of Labor Statistics, "Occupational Employment Statistics," www.bls.gov/oes/current/occ_industry.htm. Accessed January 2012.

The Telegraph, "World power swings back to America," www.telegraph.co.uk/finance/comment/ambroseevans_pritchard/8844646/World-power-swings-back-to-America.html. Accessed January 2012.

Mike Schüssler and Jasson Urbach, "The Economic Impact of Cloud Computing in South Africa," The Freemarket Foundation, Johannesburg, www.freemarketfoundation.com/DynamicData/Event_45.pdf.

Federico Etro, "The Economic Consequences of the Diffusion of Cloud Computing," 2010 World Economic Forum, The Global Information Technology Report 2009–2010.

Sustainable Industries, "Sustainability in the Cloud," http://sustainableindustries.com/articles/2011/01/sustainability-cloud. Accessed January 2012.

Carbon Disclosure Project, "Cloud Computing: The IT Solution for the 21st Century," http://content.yudu.com/A1t6nj/Cloud-Computing. Accessed January 2012.

Environmental Leader, "CDP Cloud Computing Can Save $12bn," www.environmentalleader.com/2011/07/20/cdp-cloud-computing-can-save-12bn. Accessed January 2012.

Verdantix, "Verdantix Cloud Computing Report For Carbon Disclosure Project Forecasts $12.3 Billion Financial Savings For US Firms," www.verdantix.com/index.cfm/papers/Press.Details/press_id/58/verdantix-cloud-computing-report-for-carbon-disclosure-project-forecasts-12-3-billion-financial-savings-for-us-firms/-. Accessed January 2012.

The World Community Grid, www.worldcommunitygrid.org. Accessed January 2012.

Information Week, "Eli Lilly on what's next in the cloud," www.informationweek.com/cloud-computing/blog/archives/2009/01/whats_next_in_t.html. Accessed January 2012.

BioPharma News, http://biopharmadirectory.com/news/?p=159. Accessed November 2011.

Amazon Web Services, "Global Solution Providers," http://aws.amazon.com/solutions/global-solution-providers. Accessed January 2012.

Lawn, Philip A., "A theoretical foundation to support the Index of Sustainable Economic Welfare (ISEW), Genuine Progress Indicator (GPI), and other related indexes," *Ecological Economics* 44 (2003) 105/118, Elsevier, 2003.

UNDP, Human Development Reports, "Human Development Index (HDI)," http://hdr.undp.org/en/statistics/hdi. Accessed January 2012.

Korten, David C. "Path to a Just and Sustainable New Economy," Revised and expanded version of a presentation delivered to The EU Club of Rome, Brussels, January 26, 2010. Available at www.neweconomictheory.org/content/background-papers. Accessed February 2012.

Works Consulted

Andersen, Benedict. *Imagined Communities: Reflections on the Origin and Spread of Nationalism.* London: Verso, 1993.

Michael Armbrust, Armando Fox, Rean Griffith, Anthony D. Joseph, Randy Katz, Andy Konwinski, Gunho Lee, David Patterson, Ariel Rabkin, Ion Stoica, and Matei Zaharia. *Above the Clouds: A Berkeley View of Cloud Computing*. Electrical Engineering and Computer Sciences University of California at Berkeley, Feb. 2009. Technical Report No. UCB/EECS-2009-28. Available at www.eecs.berkeley.edu/Pubs/TechRpts/2009/EECS-2009-28.html. Accessed February 2012.

Nathan Botts, Brian Thoms, Aisha Noamani, and Thomas A. Horan, PhD, "Cloud Computing Architectures for the Underserved: Public Health Cyberinfrastructures through a Network of Health ATMs." Proceedings of the 43rd Hawaii International Conference on System Sciences, 2010. Available on IEEE website, http://ieeexplore.ieee.org/xpl/mostRecentIssue.jsp?punumber=5428222. Accessed December 2011.

Carr, Nicholas (2009-01-19). *The Big Switch: Rewiring the World, from Edison to Google*. W. W. Norton & Company. Kindle Edition.

Coupland, Douglas (2010-11-30). *Marshall McLuhan: You Know Nothing of My Work!* Norton. Kindle Edition.

Cowen, Tyler (2011-01-25). *The Great Stagnation: How America Ate All The Low-Hanging Fruit of Modern History, Got Sick, and Will (Eventually) Feel Better: A Penguin eSpecial from Dutton*. Dutton Adult. Kindle Edition.

Davie, Paul. "Cloud Computing: A Drug Discovery Game Changer?" Innovations in Pharmaceutical Technology. June 2010. www.iptonline.com/synopsis.asp?cat=2&article=642. Accessed February 2012.

Ford, Martin (2009-10-05). *The Lights in the Tunnel: Automation, Accelerating Technology and the Economy of the Future*. Acculant Publishing. Kindle Edition.

Global Forum for Health Research. "Monitoring Financial Flows for Health Research: Behind the Global Numbers." October 2009.

Harms, Rolf, and Michael Yamartino. *The Economics of the Cloud*. Microsoft. November, 2010.

Hey, Tony; Tansley, Stewart; and Tolle, Kristin (2009-10-16). *The Fourth Paradigm: Data-Intensive Scientific Discovery*. Microsoft Research. Kindle Edition.

Harvey, David (2010-08-15). *The Enigma of Capital and the Crises of Capitalism*. Oxford University Press, USA. Kindle Edition.

Kolchinsky, Peter. *The Entrepreneur's Guide to a Biotech Startup*, 4th Edition. Copyright 2001, 2002, 2004 by Peter Kolchinsky.

Levy, Steven (2011-04-12). *In The Plex*. Simon & Schuster, Inc. Kindle Edition.

Max-Neef, Manfred A. *From the Outside Looking In: Experiences in 'Barefoot Economics.'* London: Zed Books LTD, 1992.

Max-Neef, Manfred A. *Human Scale Development: Conception, Application and Further Reflections.* New York: The Apex Press, 1991.

Perez, Carlota. "Finance and Technical Change: A Long-term View." *African Journal of Science, Technology, Innovation and Development.* Vol. 3, No. 1, 2011, pp. 10–35.

Prahalad, C.K. *The Fortune at the Bottom of the Pyramid, Revised and Updated 5th Anniversary Edition: Eradicating Poverty Through Profits.* Pearson Education, Inc. Upper Saddle River, NJ, 2005.

Rogers, Everett. *The Diffusion of Innovation.* New York: The Free Press, A Division of Simon and Schuster Inc., 1995.

Shahid Al Noor, Golam Mustafa, Shaiful Alam Chowdhury, Md. Zakir Hossain, and Fariha Tasmin Jaigirdar, "A Proposed Architecture of Cloud Computing for Education System in Bangladesh and the Impact on Current Education System." Department of Computer Science Stamford University Bangladesh Dhaka, Bangladesh. IJCSNS, *International Journal of Computer Science and Network Security*, Vol. 10, No. 10, October 2010.

Wu, Tim (2010-11-02). The Master Switch: The Rise and Fall of Information Empires. Random House, Inc. Kindle Edition.

B

Decision-Maker's Checklist

The following is a brief list of major items to consider before migrating a service to a cloud provider. By no means is this list comprehensive: It is merely designed to help you think through some of the most important elements in preparation for discussions with cloud computing providers. Hopefully, this basic framework will help you plan a successful migration to the cloud.

If you have suggestions for other items that should be included in this list, please feel free to post them on my website at http://cloudeconomy.in.

Quality Management

1. Are there quality initiatives—such as Kaizen, Six Sigma, or Total Quality Management (TQM)—currently underway inside my organization?

2. If so, what services are being analyzed? (List all services.)
   a. What baseline key performance indicators (KPI) are being used to measure these services?
      i. Total cost of ownership (TCO)?
      ii. Cost per user?
      iii. Availability?
      iv. Productivity?
      v. Total time to market (TTM)?
      vi. Other?

    b. Could a move to the cloud be tied to one or more of these ongoing quality initiatives? If so, would the same metrics be used to measure success? Are there other metrics that should be considered? If so, list them here.

3. If there are no quality initiatives currently under way, what are the primary metrics and KPIs used to benchmark, measure, and improve performance of departmental services?

    a. Total cost of ownership (TCO)?

    b. Availability?

    c. Productivity?

    d. Time to market (TTM)?

    e. Other?

4. What services do these KPIs measure? (List all possible services.)

5. What (if any) service-level agreements (SLA) exist for these services?

6. Given the available data regarding service delivery and availability, are there obvious areas of improvement that could be addressed by moving one or more of these services to the cloud? (List all possible services and corresponding benefits.)

7. Are these services intimately tied to other internal upstream or downstream processes? If so, could these processes be updated to support a cloud-based architecture without major architectural overhauls?

8. Who are the stakeholders that would need to support moving the selected services to the cloud? How are these individuals measured? How are their goals set? Who has responsibility for setting their goals and initiatives? (List all stakeholders and their primary concerns, goals, and vested interests.)

9. Understand all risks. What level of risk is each organization willing to tolerate as a team? Who has the most to gain from a move to the cloud? Who has the most to lose?

Architecture

1. What are the critical applications that drive your business on a daily basis? In other words, what are the applications that truly create competitive advantage in the marketplace? What applications could your business not function without?

   a. Where do these applications reside?

   b. Do service-level agreements (SLA) exist for these applications?

   c. How are they tied to upstream and downstream processes?

   d. Do these applications have business continuity/failover capabilities?

   e. How many concurrent users?

   f. How many users at peak?

2. Is there a virtualization program in place?

3. If yes, what is the current status of the migration from physical to virtual machines?

4. If yes, is there a disaster recovery/business continuity plan in place for virtual machines?

5. If no virtualization program exists today, will there be one in six months? Twelve months? Longer?

Costs

1. What is my IT organization's total cost of ownership (TCO)?

   a. Can the TCO be broken down by service?

      i. Is the storage TCO a known quantity?

      ii. Is the server TCO a known quantity?

      iii. Are there other services to consider?

   b. Can the TCO be broken down by department or application?

      i. Human Resources?

      ii. Finance?

      iii. Payroll?

2. What is the fully burdened cost of IT headcount by function? What is the full-time equivalent (FTE) cost of each individual by service? By application?

3. What are the facilities costs associated with power and cooling in the data center?

4. Regarding the services provided by your IT organization, what are the biggest cost centers?

5. What software programs are you currently licensing?

   a. How are these licenses provisioned?

   b. Is usage tracked and monitored?

   c. Does ample capacity exist to match current and anticipated growth rates?

   d. When do these licenses expire? When are they up for renewal?

6. What are the maintenance charges related to each underlying service?

   a. Storage maintenance?

   b. Server maintenance?

   c. Software maintenance?

   d. Network maintenance?

7. For each of the above maintenance contracts, when are they set to expire? When are they up for renewal?

8. What is the overall growth rate for each underlying service?

   a. What is the storage growth rate?

   b. What is the server growth rate?

   c. What is your data growth rate?

9. If a virtualization program is under way, what is the current virtual to physical (V2P) server ratio? What is the projected virtual to physical (V2P) server ratio?

Sustainability

1. Are sustainability initiatives underway in your organization? Are sustainability initiatives an area of focus for your company?

2. If so, who are the stakeholders? How will the success of these initiatives be measured? Is there a chief sustainability officer ultimately responsible for the success of these efforts?

3. Given the costs for each of the services listed previously, along with projected growth rates, is there enough data to calculate the total carbon offsets achievable by a move to the cloud?

Finance

1. What metrics does Finance use to measure project portfolio performance?

   a. Return on investment (ROI)?

   b. Payback method?

   c. Net present value (NPV)/internal rate of return (IRR)?

   d. Are there other metrics in use? (If so, list all additional metrics.)

2. Does Finance use weighted average cost of capital (WACC) with net present value analysis?

3. Is there a standard hurdle rate in use for approving new projects?

4. If one or more of the services listed previously is moved to the cloud, how will the success of the migration(s) be measured?

5. Will each migration be reviewed by Finance after completion? If so, plan to track savings as granularly as possible and at regular intervals to demonstrate returns over time (using the above metrics).

Cloud Computing

1. Are the services selected good candidates for migrating to a public cloud platform?

2. Have you evaluated offerings from multiple vendors? Have you compared pricing, basic and advanced features, and service level agreements (SLA)?

3. Are the providers' SLAs compatible with current business priorities? Are there other upstream or downstream processes that would be impacted by a cloud service outage?

4. Will the new SLAs meet or exceed current SLAs for availability, performance, and so on?

5. Factoring in for growth, will the providers' SLAs be still be acceptable one year from now? Two? If growth rates exceed your projections, will the SLAs still be sufficient, or will increases in service levels be prohibitively expensive?

Glossary

availability The amount of time a service is usable in a given time window. Often referred to in terms of "nines," as in "five nines" or "four nines availability." Five nines availability equates to 5.256 minutes of downtime per calendar year, while four nines equals 52.56 minutes of downtime per year.

bullwhip effect A supply chain phenomenon where incomplete or inaccurate information results in high variability in production outputs and typically increased costs/waste.

churn rate A company's churn rate indicates how many customers have been lost within a given time period (typically monthly, quarterly, or annually). Churn rate is one of the most important key performance indicators (KPI) for service providers.

cloud computing Computing, networking, and storage deployment and usage models designed to provide rapid time to market (TTM) and drastic reductions in capital and operational expenditures. Because cloud computing resources are provided at scale and on demand, consumers and IT end users avoid the high costs and expense associated with legacy infrastructures.

community cloud One of four cloud deployment models. In a community cloud model, more than one group with common and specific needs shares the cloud infrastructure.

cost of poor quality (COPQ) A quality measurement that refers broadly to the delta between a customer's expectations of a product (or service) and its actual performance. In the case of data center resources, COPQ can be used to quantify poor utilization rates.

direct metric A business value measurement or KPI used to measure performance of functions or processes directly related to generating revenue or financial returns.

diseconomies of scale   Relating to the production function, diseconomies of scale occur when increases to inputs result in less than proportionate increases in outputs.

economic value added (EVA)   A method devised by Stern Stewart and Company for measuring value creation:

EVA = Net operating profit after taxes (NOPAT) – (Capital * Cost of Capital)

EVA can be adjusted and applied to a single line of business or investment by changing NOPAT to net benefits.

economies of scale   Related to the production function, economies of scale occur when increases to inputs result in equivalent increases in outputs. Increasing economies of scale occur when increases to inputs result in disproportionately higher increases in outputs.

gross domestic product (GDP)   The predominant measure of economic health and progress, GDP is the value of goods and services produced by an economy. Many economists (as well as thought leaders from other disciplines) believe that the use of GDP as a measure of economic health and progress is fundamentally flawed. Other metrics, such as gross national income (GNI), are often recommended as a better indicator of quality of life.

hurdle rate   A rate typically set by corporate finance as a gate for capital investments. An investment with a projected return lower than the prescribed hurdle rate should not receive funding. A hurdle rate can be used as the discount rate in net present value (NPV) calculations to ensure that a project with a positive NPV is aligned with the company's overall investment policies.

hybrid cloud   One of four cloud deployment models, a hybrid cloud is simply a combination of two or more cloud deployment models (public, private, or community). Typically, a management framework enables the environments to appear as a single cloud for the purposes of "cloud peering" or "bursting."

indirect metric   A business value measurement or KPI used to measure the performance of functions or processes not directly related to generating revenue or financial returns.

Information Technology (IT) supply chain   The processes and functions related to the creation, assembly, and delivery of an IT service to an end user. The end user can be a paying customer or an internal employee. Processes include assigning network addresses, configuring disk storage, and creating account access. Moves, adds, and changes (MAC) are integral components of the IT supply chain.

Infrastructure as a Service (IaaS)   A cloud deployment model where the service provider delivers the necessary hardware resources (network, compute, storage) required to host and run a customer's applications. IaaS can be thought of as the inverse of Software as a Service (SaaS).

internal rate of return (IRR)   IRR can be used in conjunction with net present value (NPV) analysis. A direct metric, IRR is essentially the rate required for NPV to equal zero.

moves, adds, changes (MAC)   Fundamental functions required to provision IT services to clients, including the assignment of network addresses, disk storage, and so on.

net present value (NPV)   The NPV of an investment is the present value of all future benefits (cash flows, savings, offsets, deferrals, and so on) generated by that investment, discounted over set intervals of time, and net of any initial startup costs or investments. NPV analysis incorporates the principle of time value of money (TVM).

opportunity costs   The costs of decisions. Given scarce resources, choosing one course of action means the inability to choose other courses.

payback method   A direct metric that measures the length of time required to recoup the investment in a product or service. A product that allows the buyer to recoup his or her investment quickly is deemed a better investment than one that has a lengthy payback period.

Platform as a Service (PaaS)   One of three cloud service models, PaaS is best described as a development environment hosted on third-party infrastructure to facilitate rapid design and deployment of new applications. Google's App Engine, VMware's SpringSource, and Amazon's Amazon Web Services (AWS) are common examples of PaaS offerings.

private cloud   One of four cloud computing deployment models. Simply put, a computing environment dedicated to a single customer or tenant.

productivity   An indirect metric or key performance indicator (KPI) used to measure effectiveness and efficiency in broad strokes. Revenue per headcount is often used to gauge productivity at a very high level.

public cloud   One of four cloud computing deployment models. The public cloud deployment model is what is most often thought of as a cloud, in that it is multitenant-capable and is shared by a number of customers who likely have nothing in common. Amazon, Microsoft, Terremark, and Google, to name but a few, all offer public cloud services.

quality initiative   Quality initiatives such as Kaizen, Total Quality Management (TQM), and Six Sigma are programmatic methods of increasing corporate performance. Quality initiatives utilize KPIs as benchmarks for critical processes and as starting points for measuring improvements.

return on assets (ROA)   A direct metric that measures net income after taxes against a company's asset base. ROA is a valuable measurement but is difficult to adapt for use with internal projects.

return on equity (ROE)   A direct metric that measures returns against a company's shareholder equity. Given the use of shareholder equity, it is nearly impossible to adapt ROE for use with a single project or product.

return on investment (ROI)   A direct metric used to determine the value of an investment.

ROI = (Gains from investment – Costs of investment) / (Costs of investment)

ROI can be used with discounting to account for the time value of money (TVM). Unadjusted ROI assumes present value for all gains and costs.

service-level agreement (SLA)   A tool used to establish mutual expectations between providers and consumers of services. SLA performance is a highly useful KPI. Before selecting a cloud computing service, it is recommended that consumers review all relevant SLAs and supporting performance documentation.

Six Sigma   A well-established quality initiative that includes the DMAIC methodology (define, measure, analyze, improve, control). The term *Six Sigma* comes from statistics: A process that shows a variation of six sigma—six standard deviations from the mean—allows no more than 3.4 defects per million.

Software as a Service (SaaS) One of three cloud service models, SaaS gives users the ability to consume a software package on a service provider's infrastructure. SaaS significantly reduces the CAPEX and OPEX typically associated with owning and implementing complex software packages.

sustainability The concept that natural resources are finite and that conservation of those resources should be prioritized. Cloud computing can enable sustainable business models by dramatically reducing the carbon footprint associated with large-scale IT operations. The reductions in CAPEX and OPEX associated with cloud computing can also reduce startup costs for firms interested in building sustainable business models.

threshold hypothesis The belief that as free markets grow beyond a certain size, the related costs of that growth ultimately outweigh the benefits.

time to market (TTM) TTM measures the length of time required to implement a new application or go to market with a new service. TTM is a critical measure of a company's ability to execute. Bringing quality products to market quickly and efficiently is the simplest way to increase top-line revenue.

time value of money (TVM) TVM is the principle that money has the potential to increase in value over time—the opportunity to invest means the potential to create value. Present value and future value are measures of TVM.

total cost of ownership (TCO) The sum total of all associated costs relating to the purchase, ownership, usage, and maintenance of a particular product or service.

value chain A concept outlined by Michael Porter in his classic *Competitive Advantage: Creating and Sustaining Superior Performance*. Porter shows how firms can increase their competitive advantage in part by understanding the value of core operational and business support functions. Porter gives special attention to the concepts of economies and diseconomies of scale.

weighted average cost of capital (WACC) A measure of the cost of a company's equity and the cost of its debt after taxes.

Index